ENCOUNTERS WITH BOOKS

Teaching Fiction 11–16

DAVID JACKSON

London   METHUEN   *New York*

First published in 1983 by
Methuen & Co. Ltd
11 New Fetter Lane,
London EC4P 4EE

Published in the USA by
Methuen & Co.
in association with Methuen, Inc.
733 Third Avenue,
New York, NY 10017

© *1983 David Jackson*

Phototypeset by Tradespools Ltd,
Frome, Somerset
Printed in Great Britain by
Richard Clay (The Chaucer Press)
Suffolk

British Library Cataloguing in
Publication Data

Jackson, David, *1940–*
Encounters with books: teaching
fiction, 11–16.__
(Teaching secondary English)
1. English literature–Study and
teaching (Secondary)
–England
I. Title   II. Series
820'.7'1242   PR35
ISBN 0-416-33060-6
ISBN 0-416-33070-3 Pbk

Library of Congress Cataloging in
Publication Data

Jackson, David.
Encounters with books.
(Teaching secondary English)
1. English literature – Study and
teaching (Secondary) 2. Fiction –
Study and teaching (Secondary)
3. Youth – Books and reading.
4. Language arts (Secondary)
I. Title.   II. Series.
PR33.J32 1983   807'.12   83-1963
ISBN 0-416-33060-6
ISBN 0-416-33070-3 (pbk.)

CONTENTS

Acknowledgements p.viii

General Editor's preface p.ix

PART ONE: THE VALUE OF FICTION

1. FROM GOSSIP TALES TO WRITTEN STORY *p.*1

2. WHAT IS THE VALUE OF FICTION? *p.*7

Getting carried away, p.7; Fiction as a part of human meaning making p.8; Fiction as active confrontation, p.10; Fiction as an alternative world, p.13

3. BRINGING THE TEXT TO LIFE *p.*15

Why should a pupil be willing to participate in the reading process?, p.16; Expanding and deepening response, p.18; Stages of response, p.22; Widening the possible modes of response, p.24

4. BUILDING A CONSTRUCTIVE READING ENVIRONMENT *p.27*

Reading displays, p.27; Reading places and special reading rooms, p.32; Reading records, p.34; Reading journals, p.36; Class libraries and independent reading: catering for a variety of tastes, p.40; Setting up class libraries, p.41; Sustaining interest and helping children to choose books, p.43; Reading extracts to the class, p.44; Sharing lessons, p.49; Letters to writers, p.52; Writers in school, p.55; Other ideas, p.64

5. FRESH WAYS OF WORKING WITH TEXTS *p.67*

Improvising into a text, p.67; Designing a book cover, p.70; Deciding how to read aloud a poem/extract/story of another group, p.73; Arguing and thinking about what you read through diagrams, p.78; Keeping a reading journal, p.78; Visual interrogation (collage work), p.78; Anecdotalizing into the text, p.83; Answering in role, p.83; Detective work: group prediction methods with complete stories that make you want to read on, p.86; Alternative openings and endings in short stories, p.86

PART TWO: CASE STUDIES

Introduction p.93

6. FIRST PHASE: TRUSTING YOUR OWN VOICE IN AN UNFAMILIAR CONTEXT — 11–12+ *p.96*

Homing into The Battle of Bubble and Squeak (Philippa Pearce) through personal anecdotes, p.96; Learning to become an active reader, p.108

7. SECOND PHASE: EXPANDING
PERSPECTIVES — 1 2 + — 1 4 *p.*120

*Mastering new forms through reading and writing, p.120;
Other worlds, viewpoints, ways of living, p.149; Using multi-racial stories in an all-white school, p.154*

8. THIRD PHASE: REFLECTIVE AWARENESS —
1 4 — 1 6 + *p.*163

Dealing with a set book in literature at 16+: Great Expectations, p.163

PART THREE: FICTION FOR THE CLASSROOM

READING SUGGESTIONS FOR THE FIRST PHASE —
1 1 – 1 2 + *p.*187
CLASS LIBRARY SUGGESTIONS FOR THE FIRST
PHASE *p.*189
READING SUGGESTIONS FOR THE SECOND PHASE —
1 2 + — 1 4 *p.*191
CLASS LIBRARY SUGGESTIONS FOR THE SECOND
PHASE *p.*193
READING SUGGESTIONS FOR THE THIRD PHASE —
1 4 – 1 6 *p.*195
CLASS LIBRARY SUGGESTIONS FOR THE THIRD
PHASE *p.*197

ACKNOWLEDGEMENTS

The publishers and I would like to thank the following for permission to reproduce extracts in this book: Nina Bawden *The Peppermint Pig*, Victor Gollancz; Gwen Grant *Private, Keep Out*, William Heinemann; Gene Kemp *The Turbulent Term of Tyke Tiler*, Puffin Books; Roger McGough 'First Day at School', Jonathan Cape; Edward Lowbury 'Prince Kano', Chatto & Windus; 'Learning to Become an Active Reader', *Use of English*, Spring 1983; 'Dealing with a Set Book in Literature at 16+' *English in Education*, Spring 1982; 'Dignifying Anecdote' *English in Education*, Spring 1983; Michael Rosen for his Go-Kart poem; Liz Lochhead 'Poem for my sister' from *The Grimm Sisters*, (London, Next Editions).

I should also like to thank Peter King, an excellently supportive General Editor. More generally I should like to thank all the members of the Toot Hill Comprehensive department for their generous help, and all the pupils who taught me how to read.

GENERAL EDITOR'S PREFACE

English remains a core subject in the secondary school curriculum as the confident words of a recent HMI document reveal:—

> English is of vital importance in the development of pupils as individuals and as members of society: our language is our principal means of making sense of our experience and communication with others. The teaching of English is concerned with the essential skills of speech, reading and writing, and with literature. Schools will doubtless continue to give them high priority.
>
> (*The School Curriculum*, DES, 1981)

Such confidence belies the fact that there has been, and continues to be, much debate among practitioners as to exactly what constitutes English. If the desired consensus remains rather far off at least the interested teacher now has a large and useful literature on which he or she can profitably reflect in the attempt to answer the question 'What is English?' There have been notable books designed to reorientate teachers' thinking about the subject ranging from those absorbed by the necessary theoretical analysis, like John Dixon's *Growth Through English* (Oxford, rev. edn 1975), to those working outwards from new research into classroom language, like *From Communication to Curriculum*, by Douglas Barnes (Penguin, 1976); but there are not so many books intended to help teachers get a purchase on their day-to-day activities (a fine exception is *The English Department Handbook* recently published by the ILEA English Centre). To gain such a purchase requires confidence built not from making 'everything new' so much as learning to combine the best from the older traditions with some of those newer ideas. And preferably these ideas have to be seen to have emerged from effective classroom teaching. The English teacher's aims have to be continually reworked in the light of new experience, and the assurance necessary to manage this is bred out of the convictions of other experienced practitioners. This is of particular importance to the new and inexperienced teacher. It is to such teachers and student teachers that this series is primarily directed.

The books in this series are intended to give practical guidance in the various areas of the English curriculum. Each area is treated in a separate volume in order to gain the necessary space in which to discuss it at some length. The aim of the series is twofold: to describe good practice by exploring the approaches and activities reflected in the daily work of an English teacher in the comprehensive school; and to give a practical lead to teachers who wish to try out for themselves a wider repertoire of teaching skills and ways of organizing syllabuses and lessons. Taken as a whole, the series does not press upon the reader a ready-made philosophy, but attempts to provide a map of the English teaching landscape in which the separate volumes highlight an individual feature of that terrain, representing its particular characteristics while reminding us of the continuity between these differing elements in the overall topography.

The series addresses itself to the 11–16 age range with an additional volume on sixth-form work, and assumes a mixed ability grouping, at least in the first two years of schooling. Each volume begins with a discussion of the problems and rationale of its chosen aspect of English and goes on to describe practical ways in which the teachers can organize their syllabus and lessons to achieve their intended goals, and ends with a brief guide to books, resources, etc. The individual volumes are written by experienced teachers with a particular interest in their chosen area and the ideas they express have been proved by them or their colleagues in their own classrooms.

It is at the level of the practical that any synthesis of the various approaches to English can be gained, and to accomplish this every teacher must be in possession of a rationale and an awareness of good methods wherever and however they have been achieved. By reading the books in this series it is to be hoped that teachers will be encouraged to try out for themselves ideas found effective by their colleagues so gaining the confidence to make their own informed choice and planning in their own classrooms.

Peter King
July 1983

PART ONE
THE VALUE OF FICTION

1

FROM GOSSIP TALES
TO WRITTEN STORY

Miss Dugdale, after we 'ad prayers in the big hall, she'd go round an' look at yer shoes, then she'd say, 'About turn', we'd about turn an' she'd look at the back of yer shoes. If you 'ad dirty shoes, 'No play. Stay in'. Well, very often our parents never 'ad enough money to buy boot polish so we used to spit on a brush to put on our shoes. Then she'd say, 'Hands out'. You'd 'ave to put yer hands out an' yer nails 'ad to be clean an' yer hands to be clean. She was a perfect governess, that one. If you only walked in front of 'er desk, you 'ad to say, 'Please excuse me, Miss Dugdale'. She'd nod and you were allowed to pass 'er desk.

One time, it was a girl's birthday an' there was three of us, like friends, an' one girl, she kept a fried fish shop, said to me, 'I'm going to give Lily Hopkins a present'. I said, 'Oh how nice', and thought to meself she didn't give me anythin'. So anyhow, we were sat one in front the other like an' she said, 'Lily, 'ere's a present'. So Lily caught 'old the present an' put it underneath 'er desk an' she looked back at me. 'I've got a present'. So she undone it, it was a raw plaice. So of course we started laughin' an' I used to laugh rather hearty, an' teacher said, 'Come out'. Lily Hopkins goes out with this fish behind 'er back an' of course all the class then started roaring laughin'. Well, governess was in the other room. She 'eard us laughin' an' out she came. 'What's going on here?' Teacher said, 'Lily Hopkins has had a present from Kate Simmons and she's brought her in this fish'. 'Oh', she said, 'you horrible things. Go to my room.' We went to 'er room, we each 'ad two cuts with the cane an' it wasn't really nothin' to do with me. Then we 'ad to go out and put pinafores over our head. She'd stand us in the corner. We were shamed then. And of course when we 'ad our pinafores over our head we used to catch 'old an' peep out the corner an' make all the rest laugh. We were proper hardened at school, mind. Anyhow, we all 'ad the cane for Kate Simmons bringin' the fish to school for Lily Hopkins, so Mrs Hopkins thought it wasn't right. Course, my mother never took no notice, she said 'You ought to behave yourself. Serve you good right.' Didn't get no sympathy. But Lily Hopkins's mother goes up an' it was beltin' down with rain an' she 'ad an old pair of slippers on. She knocked on the door. She said, 'Which is Miss Waite? What do you mean by caning my girl?' Miss Waite was over in the corner.... She took off 'er slipper an' she slung that slipper across at 'er an' there was the mark of the dirty slipper on the wall. Well, governess said she'd send for the police an', oh, we 'ad a lecture. Some gentleman, I don't know who he was, came to the school an' gave us all a lecture saying' that if anythin' happened like that again, we'd all get put in homes an' our fathers and mothers 'ud be summonsed. Frightened us to death. When we used to get the cane after that we never used to go home an' tell. (DAISY WINTLE)[1]

We all live in a world of tales. Like Daisy Wintle's tale about schooling in Bristol in the 1900s we share our sense of ourselves and the world through small, personal stories. As soon as we open our mouths in playground, workplace, home or pub we move naturally towards salvaging the past or recent present through gossip tales. Indeed, it is our spontaneous way of making ourselves more visible to ourselves and others. Gossip tales seem casually entertaining but they are also intimately tied in to our sense of identity, our dignity and self respect.

Although these gossip tales often sound factually accurate they are more at home in the world of fiction. Daisy Wintle's memory tale is from an actual incident but it has been selected and re-cast in the light of how she sees herself and the world outside at the present moment of time. (So her personal sense of sticking up for herself against a regimented, educational routine provides the shaping focus for the selection of the fish story, her own hearty laugh and the peeping from behind pinafores.)

Gossip tales come to us as a primary, human necessity,[2] as a way of tailoring down the otherwise bewildering flux of experience to our own personal sizes, and what we can bear to live with. To make sense of a volatile world we regularize its randomness into the comparative order of gossip tales. Everyday we carry them around inside the head as 'mental maps' and attempt to come to terms with the unexpectedness of actual experience by placing it in relation to these story maps, so that later the original maps have to be slightly modified or revised.

Viewed from this angle, fiction stops being the stuff we find only in books. In order to live we have to make fictions. It's one effective way of patterning the chaos of experience. And instead of fiction being seen as an exclusively literary thing, isolated hierarchically from the Daisy Wintle type of spoken anecdotes, all these arbitrary divisions can merge into the more connected workings of a fiction-making continuum that holds together gossip tales, diary anecdotes and book fiction.

The writer is a part of the community of tale tellers,

gathering material from the same source as Daisy Wintle did. But whereas gossip tales can sometimes appear meanderingly casual, raw, free-wheeling, writers often refine spontaneous tale-telling into the wider needs of significant form and an expanded audience. So that the writer carries further the fiction-making process that we noticed in the Lily Hopkins birthday story; heightening, organizing, rearranging, selecting, omitting, inventing and generally working up random incidents into a more telling shape.

We can detect this movement within the fiction-making continuum in the work of several writers.

The written-up anecdotes found in the diary and journal impressions of writers like Francis Kilvert hint at an intermediary stage within this general drift.[3] Some of Kilvert's shared tales seem deceptively simple and casually matter-of-fact at first meeting as if they have just been snatched from the lips of one of the members of his parish community, like Mr Wall's account of William Jones' suicide:

At noon on Saturday Rachel's step-children missed him. They had seen him go towards the barn some hours before. They went and looked through a lancet hole of the old building and saw the old man lying on the floor, and they came back saying that old William Jones was lying in the barn dead. The master and I went down to the barn. Inside the barn there was a door leading into a beast house. The old man could not shut the barn door from the inside, so he had gone into the beast house and had shut himself in. Then he had leaned his stick up in a corner quite tidy. He had then taken out a razor, unsheathed it, putting the sheath back into his pocket. He was lying on the floor on his face when we saw him. The master turned him over. Heaven send I never see such a sight again. His head was nearly cut off, both arteries were cut through, the tongue was unrooted and, (perhaps in his agony), he had put his hand into the wound and torn his 'keck' and everything out.[4]

But on further reflection the disguised artifice of the shrewdly composed structure of the tale becomes clear, with its arranged build up from the distance of the 'lancet hole' view through to the fully developed horror of the dramatic climax.

Or take an opening for a story like the one in *The Peppermint Pig* by Nina Bawden:

> Old Granny Greengrass had her finger chopped off in the butcher's when she was buying half a leg of lamb. She had pointed to the place where she wanted her joint to be cut but then she decided she needed a bigger piece and pointed again. Unfortunately, Mr Grammett, the butcher, was already bringing his sharp chopper down. He chopped straight through her finger and it flew like a snapped twig into a pile of sawdust in the corner of the shop. It was hard to tell who was more surprised, Granny Greengrass or the butcher. But she didn't blame him. She said, 'I could never make up my mind and stick to it, Mr Grammett, that's always been my trouble.'

On first impression it sounds like the spontaneous utterance of a family anecdote worn smooth by generations passing it on, but then the awareness of the fine timing, the dramatic emphasis and the concluding proverbial wisdom makes the reader think of the writer working on it so that it fits into a wider framework of artifice.

And then again there is John Branfield's *The Fox in Winter* where the method of tale telling used to excavate Tom Treloar's past is mainly through an impression of transcribed anecdote. Fran, a 16-year-old girl in Cornwall, comes to terms with her anxieties about 'old people and pain and emotion' by slowly getting to know Tom's buried life through his 'stories of birds and animals and the sea'. Through Tom sharing and displaying objects and related anecdotes about the seal cave, woodcocks, a rabbit's paw, brass objects rescued from a wreck, the Cornish tin miners' game of Fox and Geese, the meeting with the boy from St Kitts, etc., he is able to salvage something from the collapsing dignity he feels in becoming physically incapable. The anecdotes exist simultaneously in their own right (reminding the reader of the vivacity of the spoken telling) and are also an inseparable part of the overall design of the novel. Instead of being split apart, both anecdote and the more conscious written framework of the book mingle with each other, supporting each other, both coming from the mental storehouse of accumulated gossip tales but developed in different ways. We need to go on recognizing and celebrating the common root of fiction-making in our work in the classroom.

Notes

1   Stephen Humphries, *Hooligans or Rebels? An Oral History of Working Class Childhood 1889–1939*, Oxford, Basil Blackwell, 1981.
2   Barbara Hardy, 'Towards a poetics of fiction', in Margaret Meek, Aidan Warlow and Griselda Barton (eds), *The Cool Web*, London, Bodley Head, 1977.
3   In relation to this intermediary stage consider Ronald Blythe's poetic editing of spoken anecdote, especially in episodes like 'The Victorian Gardener' and 'The Gravedigger' from *Akenfield*, Penguin (1966) which are more like fictional representations of fact, and Jane Gardam's use of oral community tales in 'The Hollow Land', Julia MacRae Books (1981) where she sets them within a formal tapestry.
4   W. Plomer (ed.), *Kilvert's Diary*, Harmondsworth, Penguin, 1977.

2

WHAT IS THE VALUE
OF FICTION?

Getting carried away

'Sometimes when I'm really enjoying the book I get carried away and picture myself in that position'. (Nicola Wood)

Fiction can wholly engross us – our feelings, imaginations, thoughts – like no other reading can. Timetables, recipes, instructions, programmes are useful and we need to be able to understand them as we make our own way in the world but powerful fiction can haunt us. Reading experiences like *The Midnight Fox* (Betsy Byars), *The Shadow Cage* (Philippa Pearce) and *The Wizard of Earthsea* (Ursula le Guin) can possess us and 'carry us away'.

With a bit of luck and the sustained support of home and school, good fiction can, at times, penetrate into the inner life of the child. It can speak most memorably, intensely and pleasurably to children's developing concerns and purposes, and it can also have a strong, motivating force. Whereas regular worksheets tend to flatten interest, lively fiction has a unique power to provoke children's curiosities, puzzlings,

guesses about the reasons why people act, speak and behave
in the way that they do. Unlike more abstract, distanced
contexts, fiction deals in particular scenes where people
respond directly and immediately to one another. And so like
Nicola 'picturing herself in that position', many children are
motivated by these kinds of specific encounters to engage
themselves more fully and more personally in the life of the
book.

These incentives can also generate a rare willingness in the
child to want to reflect upon and search for meaning in what
she reads. They can mark a shift in the child from being docile
in front of print to the child wanting to see herself in the new
role of constructive reader and thinker. As the third-year
pupils remark in their work on *I am The Cheese* (Robert
Cormier) below:

> Lindsay ... you just read it ... and the story just goes on
> from there ... but this story doesn't just unfold.
>
> Mandy   You have to unfold it yourself.

This can lead on to the child creating her own personal
contexts for the print on the page, establishing new connections and relationships between what she knows already and
the world of the book and developing the ability and
preparedness to articulate questions about what she's read
that arise from genuine gaps in understanding.

All this engaged absorption in the world of the book might
not morally improve the child, but it can lead, if the context is
right, to what L.C. Knights calls 'a quickening of the consciousness'.[1]

Fiction as a part of human meaning making

Fiction can also help us to survive in a chaotic world. The
story form is one of the ways we have of imposing a satisfying
pattern upon the disconnected impressions of actual experience. From an early age children are learning to gain mastery

over the internal rules and conventions of story patterns.[2] They begin to recognize and anticipate the rules of the game being employed in different stories. Stories like the regular, alternating patterns of contrasting reality and fantasy in John Burningham's *Come Away from the Water, Shirley*, the symmetrical repetition of *Not now Bernard* by David McKee which when applied to a monster and not a small boy produces the humour, and the ironic inversion of rules governing expected endings in stories like 'And I mean it Stanley' by Crosby Bonsall (*Early I can read book*) and 'The Thrush Girl' by Godfried Bomans (*The Yellow Storyhouse*).

Raw experience often dazes children with its 'humanly uninteresting successiveness' and 'one damn thing after another', whereas stories can create a coherent unity between beginnings, middles and endings. Readers, with their informed sense of shaped patterning, or sense of story, learn to construe isolated incidents or episodes in stories, as they do in life, in terms of a simultaneous awareness of what has gone before and what is going to happen next. So that single events are organized in the reader's head, in the light of her sense of story, into an overall pattern of significance. In this sense a growing awareness of structural coherence is the same as being able to make meaning out of books and the confusing sprawl of happenings, in the world outside.

Humanly a sense of significant pattern (gained from years of actively experiencing and participating in stories) is one of our most neglected mental systems through which we make sense of ourselves and our place in the world. By reference to this system we are able to edit down the experience of a flickering night journey by train, our past memories of a childhood place, a few evenings spent watching 'Coronation Street' or 'Brookside', into more manageable shapes. We all make meaning out of experience by regularizing it into some kind of coherent order, and fiction can make a valuable contribution to these ordering and organizing mental strategies.

The detailed work below on 'The secret life of Walter Mitty' and *Great Expectations* (p 19; pp 163–82) also shows how an appreciation of the underlying connecting thread in a story is interwined with the way the reader makes meaning out of the story through her own efforts. So that in both literature and life a developed sense of pattern and shaped order can help people to cotton on to what is going on.

Fiction as active confrontation

Without wanting to claim too much for fiction, nevertheless it can, if selected and handled shrewdly enough, be a contributory force in helping children to challenge and call into question the conditioning processes that have shaped their customary opinions, attitudes and beliefs.

Many television and reading experiences deal with stock reactions, fearing to take on any approach or subject that might be seen as controversial or offensive. In doing so they merely 'reinforce the given life of the times' and therefore 'dare not genuinely disturb the status quo'.[3] Here I am not just thinking of the most extreme examples of books that encourage in children a docile acquiescence to the status quo, such as that found in W.E. Johns's Biggles books, which teach that decent behaviour wins in the end *as a natural order of things* ('I teach the spirit of teamwork, loyalty to the crown, the Empire and to *rightful authority*'),[4] but more subtle, contemporary cases.

On the surface Judy Blume (author of, *Are You There, God? It's Me, Margaret*; *It's Not The End of the World* and *Then Again, Maybe I Won't*) seems to be encouraging a healthy openness and independent-mindedness in children having to pick their own way through the traumas and fears of growing up in New Jersey, America. Indeed some of her books, such as *Tales of a Fourth Grade Nothing*, do have an immediacy that children warm to. In *Are You There, God? It's Me, Margaret* she deals directly, and often humorously, with the problems of flat-chestedness, the embarrassment of buying your first bra, wanting to menstruate as soon as all the other girls in your gang, kissing pillars as a practice for the real thing, etc.; but although it appears, at times, to be valuing independent choice in children (like being able to choose about religion in your own way rather than merely following your parents' wishes), on a deeper level the book does not attempt to question the glossy, conformist values that are at the heart of the reading experience.

In a self-satisfied and self-preoccupied suburban background of lawn-sprinklers, Granny going on cruises, and swimming pools, Margaret (the book's narrator) is initiated into a value system that includes defining yourself as a physically attractive object trying to gain the approval of boys ('You'll want everybody to see you. Like those girls in *Playboy*'), where the gang keep Boy Books ('which was a notebook with a list of boys' names in order of how we liked them') and where normality is viewed as having to fit in to the current New Jersey values of competitive individualism and fast, sleek living. The world of *Charlie's Angels* is not too far away as a model for Margaret to aspire to.

Against the example of the fictions that perpetuate 'the given life of the times', some fictions can, more resiliently and disturbingly, confront and call into question the habitual, unthinking values of young readers. If carefully chosen and approached through active-interrogation teaching methods (like the group prediction on the perplexing ending of *The Turbulent Term of Tyke Tiler* included in the case study 'Learning to become an active reader' below, p. 108), poems like 'The Choosing' (Liz Lochhead) from *Strictly Private*, chosen by Roger McGough, and stories like *It's My Life* (Robert Leeson) can provoke children to stand back from their automatic reactions and question those habitual values. If given time and the right context to talk (in undirected groups) about a book like *It's My Life*, 14-year-olds (such as the ones included in the following transcript) can sometimes move beyond a stock response to a more profound re-considering of some of their customary attitudes:

H.   ... he [Jan's father], said that she could bung in her exams and that ... because he wanted her at home to do all the work.

J.   ... I think he felt that ... him going back to school was more important than her getting her exams.

H.   ... didn't he realize it was Jan's Mum too ... he never considered her feelings at all ... it was just the little lad.

J.   I think he should have been straight with him at the beginning and told him what had happened.

H.   ... fancy telling him that his Mum had gone on holiday.

H.W. ... how often do Mums go on holiday on their own then?

H.   ... and then her Dad seemed to be worried about Kevin's school work and everything ... Jan's got to study for her exams ... she's got all the housework to do ... and he never seemed to realize that she might be upset ... I don't think he was once kind or considerate ... about her Mum ... to her.

This book revolves around the sudden disappearance of Mum, and the resulting choices confronting her 16-year-old daughter Jan about whether to prop up the collapsing household by becoming a substitute Mum, or to concentrate on her O-levels and her own career.

These 14-year-olds are having to revise some of their stereotypical expectations about 'A mother's place is in the home' in reflecting together on the book. Recoiling against the male-dominated assumptions that control the book's household ('Kevin's got to have his breakfast and tea and his hand held at night, you've got to have your cups of tea, your clean shirt and your nice dinner on Sundays with Gran's lovely apple crumble'), the pupils are on their way to challenging the traditional expectations about the domestic, subordinate role of women. In a small but significant way fiction can help children to question and attack distorted viewpoints and second-hand opinion.

Fiction as an alternative world

Reading starts with our withdrawal from the immediate buzz of life. It can founder there by being used as a regular, escapist retreat. But it can also, when things go well, return to offer a new dimension on our usual patterns of living and to strengthen our grip on our sense of life's possibilities.

'You can get away in another kind of place', and '[reading] helps [pupils] to break off from the world and get deep into the lives of the people they're reading about' remark two second-year pupils in a recent reading survey that I carried out. They are right in so far as the reader's absorption in a good read partly comes from the sense of being able to overcome the immediate, physical limitations of time and place and being able to investigate what might have been rather than what is.

As Margaret Meek says, 'We gain more lives than one, more memories than we could ever have from what happened to us: in fact, a whole alternative existence, in our own culture or that of others.'[5] But only if we can bind together what we already know with the fresh reading encounter, so that both worlds illuminate each other. By trying ourselves out in different positions, cultures and worlds through our reading we can, when we are actively engrossed, gain new understanding of, and perspectives on, ourselves and our place in the world. But again only if we are able to relate these new experiences to our already existing system for making sense of these fresh perspectives. The sectarian hatred and prejudices in Belfast explored in *Under Goliath* (Peter Carter) will remain blank to us if we cannot come to terms with them through our familiar, daily perceptions of prejudice within our own families, local communities and social contexts.

For a much more developed treatment of some of the problems and contradictions involved in this area, see the case study below on 'Other worlds, points of view, ways of living' (p. 149) and particularly the pupils' responses to 'Free Dinners' by Farrukh Dhondy (p. 156).

Notes

1   'Literature and the teaching of literature', in L.C. Knights (ed.), *Explorations 3*, Harmondsworth, Penguin, 1979.
2   See M. Meek, *Learning to Read*, London, Bodley Head, 1982.
3   *Speaking to Each Other*, Vol. 1: *About Society*, by Richard Hoggart, London, Chatto & Windus, 1970.
4   W.E. Johns, quoted in Geoffrey Trease, *Tales Out of School*, London, Heinemann, 1964.
5   Meek, op. cit.

3

BRINGING THE TEXT TO LIFE

The print on the page starts to stir and come to life at the point where the reader begins to remake the text inside his own head. Meaning is not hidden away within the text for the reader to discover by the mechanical application of a practical criticism approach (although sensitive close reading can help) but is produced by the reader setting up a 'live circuit'[1] between her own perceptions and the text.

Instead of the teacher telling the child what to think and feel about what she is reading (however indirectly that might be done) her job changes to one of encouraging constructive conversations, or interactions between young readers and texts. And that often entails a corresponding change in the physical organization of the classroom, moving away from rows of desks/tables facing the front to small clusters of tables facing each other, or a rectangular boardroom arrangement without the teacher necessarily having a special desk and chair.

The new reading experience has to be actively fitted into the child's already existing networks of understanding through her own efforts for the experience to become a part of the child. And that often implies some kind of shift or rearrangement of the existing networks in the process. To give some specific examples here, the group of children in the case study below ('Learning to become an active reader', p. 108) have to reinterpret their habitual expectations in order to understand the surprise ending of *The Turbulent Term of Tyke Tiler*. And again, in reading *The Midnight Fox* (Betsy Byars) the 11-year-old pupils reshaped that experience in terms of what they knew and expected.[2] They did not read or see the book as the teacher did but construed it in the light of their own narrative anticipations so that they remade the teacher's ideas as he in turn was forced to rethink theirs. By the time the book was finished both the book itself and the activities in which the teacher and pupils had jointly engaged were understood in ways which neither teacher nor children had previously envisaged.

So what matters most in trying to bring the text to life in the classroom is whether the teacher can both encourage the child to participate actively in the reading process, and value and respect children's latent powers of understanding in the way the book is approached in the classroom.

Why should a pupil be willing to participate in the reading process?

Imaginative literature, more than any other kind of text[3], has the motivating strength to engage pupils' interests. Fiction like *The Bakerloo Flea* (Michael Rosen), *Flowers for Algernon* (Daniel Keyes), *The Basketball Game* (Julius Lester), 'The Place' (John Gordon) from *The Spitfire Grave and Other Stories*, and *Sliding* (Leslie Norris) have the ability to activate a rare preparedness in children to want to participate in the reading encounter.

This willingness to be involved in a text also hinges upon the amount of pleasurable involvement that children find in it.

Fiction can also tune in to the special wavelengths and emotional preoccupations of children at particular ages. A short story like 'The End of Something' by Hemingway can link up with the specific, felt concerns and interests of pupils between the ages of 14 and 16 with their curiosities about boy/girl relationships, splitting/breaking up, the difficulties of loss, grief and separation, and (besides the local fascination with the details of a fishing trip) personal choices about identity, for example, the questioning within Nick about whether he is a person who needs to concentrate on hunting with Bill, or loving with Marjorie.

The other important aspect of this willingness is the way that certain kinds of fractured, dislocated fictions can often excite pupils to actively engage with the text. Iser has pointed out that deliberate interruptions, breaks and gaps in a reader's understanding when moving through a text can often 'bring into play our own faculty for establishing connections – for filling in the gaps left by the text itself'.[4]

The planned uncertainty of a non-linear fiction like *I am The Cheese* (Robert Cormier), or *Red Shift* (Alan Garner), can, if the approach is set up properly, provoke the young reader's already existing processing devices to seek out coherent links between the apparently unrelated fragments of the fiction. So, for example, the surprising juxtaposition of the cycle, tape and childhood flashback stories in *I am The Cheese* (see the case study below, 'Mastering new forms through reading and writing', p. 120) triggers off pupils' searchings for meaning in what they read, because it generates the need to work out independently a coherent web of meaning that explains to themselves what they thought was going on in the book.

The way a teacher works in the classroom (in terms of style, context and approach) can also affect the pupil's learning stance within it. The examples contained in the section 'Fresh ways of working with texts' are all a part of trying to change the customary, passive role of the child to that of a challenging participator in reading activities. They need to be tried out, revised and added to, according to the different kinds of interaction produced by different classroom environments.

Expanding and deepening response

Although meaning is gained through an act of active participation by the reader that does not mean to say that the text is unimportant. Indeed, the text can only be brought fully alive through a joining of the reader's response with an awareness of the internal conventions and narrative structures being employed within the text.

Traditionally we have been much stronger in Britain on reader response than the structural mechanics of the text. Perhaps what is needed now, in more and more English classrooms, is not to exaggerate the importance of either strand, but to discover for ourselves the possibilities of fusing both approaches in the child's quest for meaning in what she does. So the concern with how a child gains progressive mastery over the tacit rules, systems and conventions of fiction should go hand in hand with some of the approaches designed to elicit pupil response outlined below. Learning about the grammar of stories (see the case study 'Mastering new forms through reading and writing' below, p. 120) is an integral part of the reader's construction of meaning from what she reads. As David Lodge remarks, 'the structural coherence of narratives is inseparable from their meaning, and reading them is inseparable from forming hypotheses about their overall meaning'.[4] Making meaning out of what she reads is for a story reader a unitary competence. It is not just about attending to detached, single extracts, phrases or episodes but a creative mental act of piecing together those single units into a common, unifying arrangement, in the light of the reader's dawning awareness of the story's overall design.

The reader casts backwards and forwards in the story at the

same time, making meaning by actively building inside her head a coherent unity that ties together the beginning, the middle and the ending of the story. Each separate story event is bound up with a sense of what has gone before and what is going to happen next in the reader's mind so that through the interweaving of anticipations and retrospections a whole pattern of meaning is formed. Therefore learning more about narrative structure and learning to become a more effective reader and meaning-maker are the same process.

One brief example might sharpen up the point. In working with James Thurber's short story, 'The secret life of Walter Mitty' it is obviously important to help the pupils, say 14–16-year-olds, to a deeper, personal response and understanding of the text by inviting them to explore their own daydreaming/reality stories and anecdotes, but this can turn out to be a flabby idea if the pupils are not encouraged to base their own comic improvisations on a conscious appreciation of the structural correspondences that exist within the text.

So before the pupils are asked to work on their stories, a preliminary space and time needs to be given over to activities that will help them to discover the overall design of the story for themselves. Divided up into small groups I asked them to discuss and make notes in their reading journals on the following question: 'What are the connecting threads (e.g. similarities, repetitions, linked clues) between the daydreaming pieces and the real life pieces in the story that help you to understand what's going on?'

All the group had a chance to sort out the divisions between the fantasy episodes and the actual world in the process of doing this. Most of them referred to the surface repetitions of the 'pocketa-pocketa-pocketa' noise, and more significantly to the connecting clues that immediately precede the daydreaming parts, like the reference to the hospital that prompts the operation on the millionaire banker, the newsboy shouting about the Waterbury trial that gives rise to the scene in the courtroom, and the article in a copy of *Liberty* (heavy-handed

irony?) on 'Can Germany conquer the world through the air?'
that activates the flying scene.

But the group were more varied in their reactions and less
confident in their handling of the main structural correspondences between the fantasy/real world juxtapositions. The
compensatory experience of authoritative power and domination of the fantasy super-hero figures of his imagination (e.g.
Commander of the Navy hydroplane, expert surgeon, crack
shot and super criminal, flying ace) showing up the cowardice
or inadequacy of Lieutenant Berg, Drs Renshaw, Bendow and
Remington, Mr Pritchard-Mitford, the District Attorney and
young Raleigh, are put against the recurringly humiliating
experiences in the actual world (e.g. his wife nagging about
him driving too fast, the parking lot attendant belittling him,
the bathos of 'Puppy Biscuit' being overheard by a passing
couple, and the angry remonstrance of his wife again).
Nobody in the group had discerned any critical differences in
treatment between the first four day-dreaming episodes
(hydroplane, hospital, courtroom, flying scene) and the concluding scene of the firing squad.

Walter Mitty uses the first four daydreams to cope with the
harassing pressures of his wife, and although it is an
unhealthy, escapist retreat the reader does not sense that it is a
pathological habit. But the final fantasy is signalled as being
different in kind to the reader. It is the only time in the story
that Mitty tries to do something independent *in the real
world*. 'Does it ever occur to you that I am sometimes
thinking?' he ventures, but is squashed flat again by his wife's
finger-wagging, 'I'm going to take your temperature when I
get you home.'

This last fantasy scene is not signalled by a connecting clue,
as in the others. There is no connecting bridge between the
real and the fantasy worlds. The boundaries between both
worlds dissolve and Mitty is left with the hollow pretence of a
defiant gesture ('erect and motionless, proud and disdainful,
Walter Mitty the undefeated, inscrutable to the last') that

hints to the reader that he has permanently withdrawn from the injuries of the real world, a psychically crippled wreck.

Something like this awareness of structural similarity and dissimilarity within the text can help the reader to organize the separate threads of the story. In trying to cotton on to the overall structural design of the story the pupils were having to synthesize their random reactions as readers into more coherent systems of meaning. So bringing together a concern for narrative structure with the readers' personal responses can help the text to be brought more fully alive within the classroom.

Experiencing the text comes before formal analysis. Living with it, browsing with it, carrying it into your own world of feeling and thinking and having the time, right context, and space to allow the text to make unpredictable demands on you, the reader, is what must come first.

Too often the young reader is cut off from these early, open encounters by the classroom emphasis on parrot talk and 'critic talk'. As Robert Witkin remarks, 'Too often what passes for creative response to works of literature is merely stylized analysis, predictable and elaborated critic talk.... English teachers are often responsible for reinforcing verbal behaviour of this kind.... It's a passport to success in examinations. Critic talk is exam talk so far as the English teacher is concerned and, since critics must have something to talk about, works of literature are delivered as grist for their mills.'[5]

So pupils need more time to move with the unfolding energies of the text so that they can find their own ways of gaining entry and perhaps possessing the reading experience for themselves. Ways like setting up a role play context to explore some of the issues in *Midnight is a Place* (John Aiken),[6] burying the time capsule as a way into *The Midnight Fox* (Betsy Byars), tape-recording people's everyday memories of the Second World War as a way of contextualizing *Carrie's War* (Nina Bawden), an oral history, autobiography/biogra-

phy project within the community as a way of working with
The Fox in Winter (John Branfield), using drama to engage
with some of the central experiences in *Z for Zachariah*
(Robert C. O'Brien), or a visual interrogation project with the
poem 'Prince Kano' (Edward Lowbury) (see 'Fresh ways of
working with texts' below, p. 67).

Despite the occasional evidence of lively, open approaches,
pupils are frequently taught not to trust in their own
perceptions but obediently to swallow instructions about
what to think and feel delivered from the front of the
classroom. In the later years they are too often nudged into
parroting and borrowing a stock orthodoxy of response
because of examination pressure.

So what can teachers do about this? Ways of avoiding the
dictated notes trap and the narrowing pressures of examinations are looked at more fully in the *Great Expectations* case
study (p. 163), 'Dealing with a set book in literature at 16+'.
But, more fundamentally, one of the most healthy develop-
ments among literature teachers is the growing sign that more
of them are wanting to join in conversations and encourage
contracts of understanding within the classroom between
pupils and themselves, rather than just going on delivering
instructional lectures from on high. And along with this there
is a hesitant movement away from an exclusive concern with
teaching and how to get the Great Books across, to a new
concern with pupils' own processes of understanding through
more gradual stages of response.

Stages of response

The 'centrality of literature' approach to English, while fully
acknowledging the special power and value of literature (from
Matthew Arnold to F.R. Leavis and *Scrutiny* to Frank
Whitehead and 'Use of English') has not paid as much
attention as it should have to the child's processes of
understanding through the acts of talking and writing. A fully

articulated fusion between a language and learning method and a centrality of literature approach is urgently needed.

Elsewhere I have tried to show in detail how such a unified approach might work in practice through the establishing of three preliminary stages of response – the first encounter, coming to terms, and making a statement.[7]

The valuing of the first encounter, rather than a premature scurrying into the tight, analytical conventions of final product writing, is a key part of this more open and independent type of response. Because of its unexpectedness, and perhaps because of our special childhood receptiveness,[8] we often respond more immediately and vulnerably to those first meetings with books. It's not too rare to find some children responding with a kind of dazed wonder, or with a heightened sense of involvement.

If later critical reflection and commentary are to have any validity then we must admit and start from those first impressions. After the initial owning up to puzzlement, excitement, blockage or intense wonder, either through first-impression jottings in reading logs/journals as in the *Great Expectations* piece, or through small group talk, often sufficient momentum is generated inside the reader to carry her on to a more detailed, considered stance where commentary, intelligence and feeling can intertwine with and inform each other.

The second stage of response – coming to terms – is a complex, awkward one of balancing and reconciling different forces. The queries, speculations and impressions of the first encounter stage are a significant preliminary step in response but they need to come into contact (mainly through shared talk) with other opinions and perspectives and be modified if they are to gain a more coherent and developed shape. Through collaborative effort pupils can often build on them, or reconstruct their often sketchy first impressions, in the light of a closer look at what the text is saying, so that the meaning of the reading experience is made clearer to them. They often do this by developing a more precise sense of fit between the world of their personal hunches and the world of the book, so that disconnected first responses are pulled together into a more unified framework of understanding (see 'Thinking about the book through diagrams', p. 78).

It is not an easy journey; sometimes this expanding stage of response can collapse in apparent blockages and dead ends, but with a more constructive attitude to failure pupils can sometimes learn more about fruitful areas of possible investigation (e.g. Is that dead end in my response caused through my inadequacy or a possible flaw in the book? Am I interested enough to want to investigate further?).

Through the pupil's initial impressions, the coming to terms with other perspectives and more exact claims of the text in small group exchanges the pupil arrives (not necessarily in a sequential order) at the synthesizing, more carefully reflective stage of making a statement. The important point is that the 'Making a statement' stage (usually over-valued by schools and colleges) grows out of the early stages. Through the browsing with and provisional trying out of early feelings, impressions, blockages and ideas, a future line of enquiry might emerge that carries with it the first, raw flavour of the experience but is also modified by the process of patient teasing out of more comprehensive systems of meaning. It does not have to be a *final* statement. Pupils can go back and continuously revise, but it does represent a more considered bringing together of informed feeling with passionate thinking.

Widening the possible modes of response

Along with this expansion of response through linked stages goes a related widening of the possible modes of response available to the pupil. Given some kind of bargaining relationship within the classroom, and an occasional opportunity for the pupil to select and choose for herself, a greater variety of response can be fostered.

Tape recording, collage work, improvised drama, role play, strip cartoons and all the detailed suggestions included in 'Fresh ways of working with texts' (below, p. 67) are valuable ways of coming at texts in the classroom. But what is centrally important in all this is the way certain pupils can, if given a long enough familiarity with a wide repertoire of possible modes of response, select an appropriate and telling form for their developing response.

Unbidden, a sixth-form pupil produced a spider plan of the central ideas and themes of *The Grapes of Wrath* (John Steinbeck), in order to sort out her own thinking. A fifth-form boy, who had written a great deal of free verse in the early years of the secondary school, explored the connection between the prisoner out on the marshes and Pip's 'oppressed conscience' and position in the family in *Great Expectations*. A particular form, independently chosen, can allow certain things to be expressed that another teacher-approved mode might have suffocated. Finding their own way into a reading experience, if effectively supported by the teacher, can prove one of the productive ways of entering into and capturing the spirit of a reading encounter.

Notes

1 Louise Rosenblatt, *Literature as Exploration*, London, Heinemann, 1970.

2 See also 'Possessing what you read in English', in David Jackson, *Continuity in Secondary English*, London, Methuen, 1982.

3 Here I am only thinking of written texts. Television texts like 'Grange Hill' have the same power to motivate.

4 Wolfgang Iser, 'The reading process: a phenomenological approach', in Jane P. Tompkins (ed.), *Reader-Response Criticism*, Baltimore, Md, Johns Hopkins University Press, 1980.

5 David Lodge, *Working with Structuralism*, London, Routledge & Kegan Paul, 1982.
6 Robert Witkin, 'The Intelligence of Feeling', London, Heinemann, 1974.
7 Described in *Fiction as a Starting Point for Learning 8–14*, Bretton Language Development Unit 1982. Available from Colin Urch, Wakefield Education Offices, 8 Bond Street, Wakefield, West Yorkshire.
8 'Meeting books', in Mike Torbe (ed.), *Language, Teaching and Learning*, vol. 3: *English*, London, Ward Lock Educational, 1981.
9 'What do we ever get nowadays from reading to equal the excitement and the revelation of those first fourteen years?', from 'The lost childhood', in Graham Greene, *Collected Essays*, Harmondsworth, Penguin, 1981.

4

BUILDING A CONSTRUCTIVE READING ENVIRONMENT

We probably will not convince children to read in school if we do not show them, through the surroundings we create and through our examples, that reading matters personally to us. The positive example of a teacher absorbed in a book in a reading period is often more useful than any amount of exhortation. And the same applies to the general mood and atmosphere a department can build up through wall displays of pupils' responses to books, book-of-the-month exhibitions, book jacket designs, shelves of books, class libraries and odd paperbacks scattered around the teacher's desk.

Here is a range of working examples from an English department at one school that try and catch some of that attempt to set up a constructive reading environment.

Reading displays

The predictable drabness of institutional creams, greys and browns of many secondary schools often puts off many pupils. But you can learn a great deal from some of the best primary schools and their ideas on display, and that is what one Midlands school has tried to do.

As you enter the green carpeted area of the department from the library the wall displays leap out at you. It is a food topic display with a giant beefburger on the right, slurping mustard. Children's shape poems, a *Guinness Book of Food Records*, appetising alphabets brightly designed in felt-tip pen, all relieve the gloom of the windowless corridor. On the left wall a mammoth knickerbocker glory froths over, covered with mandarin oranges and pineapple slices. And there is a child's poem decorated all over with pink cherries:

Chomping cherries
Squelching round my tongue
The flesh parts and blood
pours out.
Chew, swallow.
Sweet tastes linger.

There are poster poems on the walls (Adrian Mitchell's 'Deep Sherbet' and Ted Hughes's 'Boom') and at the bottom of the stairs a special jungle scene painted onto the wall (sprouting palms, creepers, trees and creatures) with a bold poster saying:

WORDS
They talk, they read, they write
WORDS
They struggle, they read, they fight
WORDS, WORDS
They tell, they sell, they buy
WORDS
They choose, refuse, deny
W O R D S
W O R D S
W O R D S
W   O   R   D   S
W   O   R   D   S

There are two further reading wall displays on *Jacob Two-Two Meets the Hooded Fang* (Mordecai Richler) and *The TV Kid* (Betsy Byars). Framed by a black sugar-paper border, the *Hooded Fang* display is mounted on red backing paper to mask the dull walls underneath. Large letters have been cut out of black sugar-paper to silhouette the title of the exhibition. The children's work includes the unusual designs of a child power T-shirt, Mr Justice Rough's punishment book, and the rules and regulations of the children's prison. The *TV Kid* display includes a free verse poem shaped as a television with a black border and blue serrated edges set on a background of buff and black.

The secret behind all these eye-catching visuals is the departmental policy of requisitioning wallpaper rolls of backing paper (easily obtainable from local dealers) in bold, primary colours, and sugar-paper and plain paper in a variety of colours, so that with a little imagination and care, gloomy corners of classrooms or corridor space have been rescued.

Take the *Wizard of Earthsea* (Ursula le Guin) display as a central example. It is in an open area called the English lounge and most English groups have to move through this space to get to their English classroom. In many secondary schools it is such frequently used areas that get the most battering. An atmosphere of shabby neglect often discourages both teachers and children to want to try anything new, but in this particular place it is different.

The lack of formal display boards has encouraged inventiveness. Backing paper has again been used as a background to the display, trimmed around the edges with strips of black sugar-paper. The letters for the title of the book have been cut out in two colours with care, and the pupils have chosen the colours – black and purple. They decided in talking it through with the teacher that yellow would not do. It had to have an atmosphere of wizardry. So they chose black, purple and silver.

Figure 1 *The Wizard of Earthsea* display

Displays do not have to be empty decorations. They can enter into and interpret the spirit of the book. In this instance the general effect of shining aluminium foil, red paper with candlewax smeared on it and the predominant black and purple backdrop has tried to catch something of the surreal, eerie feel of the book.

Figure 2   *The Wizard of Earthsea* display

The pupils' work mounted on the display (arrived at through a gradual process of negotiation between pupils and teacher) has now been recorded on a 'possible ways of working' list to share with the other members of the department. It includes:

The display is very important, lots of room for collage and visual interpretations. Pupils who really enjoy the book can be offered *The Farthest Shore* and *The Tombs of Atuan* – the other two books in the Le Guin trilogy.

IDEAS

1 Shadow poem, using black and white paper, showing the Gebbeth and capturing its menace.
2 Retell, as a story, the challenge of the Dragon of Pendor, illustrate if you like.
3 Make a story book for the children of Earthsea about the legends, mysteries and stories of the Archipelago.

4 Who's Who in Earthsea: make a booklet.
5 The Mage's Handbook: a book of spells and curses.
6 Look at the chapter 'Hunted' (6). Write the story of the Shadow's chase from Ged's point of view (see also 14).
7 Design your own Archipelago. Invent its history, language, inhabitants, flora and fauna, etc.
8 Plan a map of Ged's voyages and write a log to go with it.
9 Write the life story of the Prince and Princess of Desolation.
10 Design- and describe the castle which houses the Terrenon.
11 The death of the Otak: write a poem and illustrate.
12 'Facing your own self – the shadow' – when you've read the last chapter, write the passage that was missed out where Ged struggles and finally overcomes the Shadow.
13 A spellbinding Quiz: children, using books, make up questions on the book and then do the quiz.
14 Look at Chapter 8, 'Hunting': write a story of chasing the Shadow from Ged's point of view.

Reading places and special reading rooms

No wonder a great many children feel restless trying to read while having to sit up behind a desk or table. It is not the most relaxed reading position and certainly not the one they feel most at home with. Most children seem to like lying flat out, or curling up in an armchair with a book, if given half a chance.

It may not be possible to encourage this kind of thing in your classroom space but often, with some inventiveness, screened-off alcoves can be made or special reading rooms constructed out of small box rooms.

As an example of what can be done just consider the special reading room at one school. It is true that there are brown stains on a part of the ceiling where water has sluiced through from burst pipes, but the first impression of the room as you enter the door is that it is a place that is looked after and valued. There is a carpet on the floor that muffles grating sounds, warm mustard anaglypta wallpaper and five large fawn and cream striped floor cushions made by the children from remnant material and collections of old tights as stuffing. An old sofa was rescued from the dustman and is now in one corner of the room with mended springs. Beside it there is an easy chair given to the department by Melanie, now in her second year. (Her mother did it up, recovering it in beige material.)

For decoration there are dried chinese lantern flowers, rubber plants, pottery pieces made by the pupils in their creative arts periods, and cow-parsley seed heads. Propped up on the long windowshelf are the departmental Story Shelf[1] collections of pupil's anecdotes, poems, jokes, riddles and illustrations, designed as 'proper books' for other children in the school to read.

Around the walls are bookcases and display racks crammed with colourful paperbacks, and in the centre of the room there is a small cluster of Formica tables with stackable chairs.

It is an adaptable room; usually children are stretched out on the cushions browsing from the Story Shelf collections and from the paperback displays, or sprawled out in the easy chair or sofa. Sometimes everybody will be reading silently, or talking about a story sitting on the chairs gathered round the tables. At other times two or three children will be sharing the jokes from the Story Shelf, or arguing noisily over some current happening.

I asked a group of 12-year-olds how they think this reading room is different from other rooms in the English department. Here are some of their remarks:

It's smaller.

You can do more work on your own.

It's quiet.

I like the cushions ... because you can read on the cushions and lounge about and all that, but in the other classrooms you've got to sit on a chair.

It's comfier ... it's better ... it's more like home ... it makes you feel you can relax.

(On the Story Shelf collections) You can see what other people's work is like ... so that when you get in the third or fourth year ... see whether you can do as well as that.

And you realize that you know that person ... so you have to read the poem ... Mick Morley looks so big now.

Reading records

Keeping accurate records of what the child is reading can be very helpful in allowing the teacher to discern patterns of development, blanks, absences, growth points, special bursts of enthusiasm and blockages. Future suggestions and guidance can be based upon this information, as in this example:

	Autumn term	*Paul 2T*
3 September	*The Goalkeeper's Revenge and Other Stories*	Bill Naughton
15 September	*Goalkeepers Are Different*	Brian Glanville
26 September	*Behind the Goal*	John Griffin
9 October	*First Season*	Roy Wilson
21 October	*Ghosts 2*	Aidan Chambers
7 November	*Nothing To Be Afraid of*	Jan Mark
14 November	*The Shadow Cage*	Philippa Pearce
28 November	*The Moon of Gomrath*	Alan Garner
6 December	*Elidor*	Alan Garner

Another approach is for the child to keep her own list of books, comics and magazines read at home and at school, with quick, personal reactions to what is read. (A more ponderous movement towards the set-piece book review with all its premature critical apparatus should be avoided.)

These lists can often give a more complete picture of the reading context ('At home I read comics in bed.') and personal attitudes, so that the teacher is put into the position of being able to act from a fuller appreciation of the child's needs and interests, and to match up a book more precisely with the child's concerns. This example is taken from the work of a 12-year-old girl just entering her second year.

A list of books read at home and school

9.11.81 At home I read comics in bed at night. Usually I read, 'The Beano', 'Jackie' or 'Photo Love'.

In the 1st year I had a lot of books from the library, but lately I don't read a lot so I've only had two books from the library this term (*On the Run, A Spell of Sleep*).

Last year I enjoyed reading *Grinny* (I don't know who it's by). And also I liked reading *On the Run* by Nina Bawden. I read some more, but those two are the two that I enjoyed and remembered most.

EDITOR	BOOK	DATE
Nina Beechcroft	*A Spell of Sleep*	15.11.81
Dianne Doubtfire	*Sky girl*	1.12.81

17.11.81 This week I changed my library books. I re-stamped one and got another by Nina Bawden (*The Witches Daughter*).

For this lesson I have signed out a book by TOPLINER called *Sky Girl*. My friend says it is a very good book, so I might get it for a library book later on. This book is by Dianne Doubtfire. (What a name!!!)

8.12.81 I have now read *Sky Girl* it certainly was a very good book. It is partly about a girl which quite a few people fancy, also it is full of adventure and excitement. I don't think I'd mind reading it again, it was fantastic!

From   I have read *Cold Christmas* which wasn't really
9.12.81   very interesting. *The Witches Daughter* was OK
to   but not really my sort of book.
23.3.82   *Tales of a Fourth Grade Nothing* by Judy Blume.
This is a really good book and I really enjoyed it,
so I decided to try to get to read all of Judy
Blume's books. Next was *Otherwise Known as
Sheila the Great* this was just as good and I was
then dying to read another of her books. Mr
Jackson then gave me another book called *It's Not
the End of the World*, this was quite sad but I
thoroughly enjoyed it. I am now reading *Are You
There, God? It's Me, Margaret*. I've nearly
finished it, I like it, but its not quite as good as the
rest of her books. (SAMANTHA)

Reading journals

As a part of a regular comment on work in progress, journal
work can open up a most productive conversation between
the child, the reading experience and the teacher.[2] It is a
chance for the child to bring in her everyday interests to meet
the world of school. Journals are often more sustained and
detailed than the usual reading record and also offer a space
for the child to share and reflect upon what is being read.

The warmth, interest and detailed advice of the teacher's
response is often crucial in reviving or motivating children's
engagement in what they are doing. Take the teacher's
reactions to the journal entries of Mark and Neil below as
examples. Neither of them sees himself in the role of confident
reader, and the teachers' comments (although a bit syrupy in
parts) confirm their out-of-school preoccupations (e.g. 'I
didn't know that *Stig* was on the TV. That's great! Do tell me
when it starts or I shall miss it.'), draw them out and offer
positive suggestions. It is that kind of continuing, relaxed
support that can make the difference between a child who can

read but does not, and the child who develops the habit of reading for pleasure.

Here are three written conversations between 11-year-olds, who have just entered the secondary school, talking to their teachers about reading.

(A) *Building bridges between the world of television and the world of the book*

Teacher Could you come and tell me why you've not started your diary please Neil.

   Pupil One of my greatest hobbies are drawing and beer mat collecting and reading when I can, especially interesting books like *Stig of the Dump* which is on television soon.

Teacher I didn't know that *Stig* was on the TV. That's great! Do tell me when it starts or I shall miss it.

          Do you know any other interesting books? Did you read any good ones at Junior School?

          What do you like drawing best, Neil?

   Pupil Well the first episode has been on Monday and it is on Wednesdays also and it was quite interesting when Barney first met Stig. (NEIL SMITH)

(B) *'It's like reading Japanize'*

   Pupil I don't like reading that much except when it's a good book. Last week I went on a bike ride I was going up a slight slope when the bike went in to slip gear my feet went down on the floor the handle bars spun round then the bike fell on top of me, now I've got a great big gravel rash.

Teacher Oh dear! Gravel rashes are *horrid* aren't they Mark? Hope it's getting better now though. I agree that reading is far more enjoyable if you've got a good book. Thank goodness we have got lots and lots of *smashing* books in the English depart- ment itself and in the Library and E8.

Pupil   The last book I read was *The Raft* I don't know who wrote it but it was a Grasshopper book, I thought it was quite good but it wasn't the best book I've read. The best book I've read was *I Am David* I thought that was brilliant. I've done six ideas on 'Jacob two two' they were the T-shirt designs. 'Mr Justice Rough's Crime Book', 'Slimmers Isle', 'The Map of the Prison', 'The Prison Catalogue' and the story about how I got in to the childrens prisons. English is my favourite lesson about, but at my other school it was the one I hated most because we did all comprehension or whatever.

Teacher   Great! I'm really pleased by this. I've always meant to read *I Am David* because several people have recommended it, now I certainly shall. What's it about?

Your Jacob 2-2 work was good. I *did* like the T-shirt. Tell me more about the horrid English at your last school – what did you do in 'Comprehension'?

Pupil   First of all in English we read a story written by Charles Dickens or another famous writer about 2 pages long in *small* print as well (worst luck) then we answered about ten questions on it like, what colour was the river when it was in flood. That's an easy one compared to some of them. Some of them was like reading *Japanize*!

I won't tell you what *I Am David* is about because it would ruin it, if you read it. All I can tell you about it is that it was very good and I would recommend it to anyone.

(MARK SCARBOROUGH)

(C) *Helping the fluent reader*

Pupil   I also enjoy reading, my best authors are Judy

Blume and Helen Cresswell. If you could possibly recommend a good book I would be very grateful. I enjoy dog walking and babies so I am very interested in dog books. I have one sister and would like a baby brother but it's not up to me. I like sports and I have been nominated the vice sports captain. When I grow up I would like to be a vet and have two Irish wolfhounds as pets. I am also very moody especially if I don't understand something. I would also like to do animal portraits. My favourite food is fish and chips. I like to imagine myself in some sort of fairy tale so half the time I live in a dream. I have run out of things to say so I think I'll stop now.

Teacher What an interesting diary Nicola! I enjoyed reading it. I'm glad you like English. What did you do in English at your Primary school? Come and chat to me about reading books and I'll find you a good one. Have you read *Tales of a Fourth Grade Nothing* by Judy Blume?

Why do you imagine yourself in Fairy Tales too? That's interesting!

P.S. I *love* fish and chips!

Pupil In English at Primary school instead of writing about books we wrote about quiz's and things like that. Even though that was quite different I like the English here too. The reading books I like are mainly stories on a certain character. I enjoy animals stories too. By the way I have read *Tales of the Fourth Grade Nothing*. The following book is called *Super-Fudge*. I have also read that and *Otherwise known as Sheila the Great* which was also written by Judy Blume. When I get moody I think it's because everything seems wrong and I get frustrated, it's normally because I've had a hard day and I've lost my temper and then I get

moody. Sometimes when I'm really enjoying the
book I get carried away and picture myself in that
position. I also do it with the television as well, I
get so excited that I find myself talking to the tele.

(NICOLA WOOD)

Class libraries and independent reading: catering for a variety of tastes

If children cannot have both a class reader and silent
reading, they prefer silent reading as they can read a book
of their own choice at their own speed, stopping to savour
or stumble, or rushing ahead as they see fit; that some
children find the book interesting, but far too slow; and
that poor readers read it aloud badly, is unbearable.
Perhaps it would be a better idea, as children get older and
books get longer, to stimulate children to read in various
ways ... with many different kinds of books, thus appeal-
ing to a wide variety of tastes ...

(JENNIE INGHAM)[3]

All children need access to both the shared class reader
experience (if selected and read effectively) and independent
reading from a class library or school library choice. It is not a
matter of 'either/or' but more a matter of a mixed, regular,
varied diet of reading styles and experiences being made
increasingly available in the life of the classroom.

No single reading strategies (like a termly class reader) can
cater for the wide-ranging diversity of pupils' tastes. Instead
what they need is something like informed departmental book
boxes (organized thematically into supernatural books, childhood and growing up, monsters, love and marriage, animals,
science fiction, humour, etc.), visiting the school library,
listening to a tape of a writer like George Layton reading his
own stories, giving children the chance to talk through what
they have read with other pupils and having a regular, class

library period. This emphasis on the pupil's voluntary reading from a class library is particularly important.

Setting up class libraries

At a time of brutal cut-back in the money and resources available to schools it is not easy to get class libraries off the ground quickly. 'The really massive and massively varied provision of books', that the Bullock report talks about to meet the healthily expanding needs of a mixed ability class demands a clear sense of priorities in coherent departmental planning over a number of years. What is needed most of all is enthusiastic commitment to the idea, an ability to persuade head teachers and English Advisers about the use of curriculum development funds and a departmental policy that does not have to waste money on expensive course books, and other irrelevancies.

One school spent a period of eight years trying to equip each English classroom with one or two book cases for a class library, and on average, at the end of this time has a range of about 50–60 paperbacks in each room, plus long term hardbacked loans from the local educational library service. This class library choice is extended every reading period by the use of one or two of the departmental book boxes (deep, moulded plastic trays that fit into shelves kept in the departmental stock room).

The choice of books is obviously crucial; years 1 to 5 all select from these book cases so an extremely wide variety of subject matter, style, voice and textual complexity is needed. Reluctant or insecure readers deserve a great deal of careful thought here. The department of this school agrees with the ILEA English Centre booklet on *Class Libraries: Work with Five Classes* when it says, 'it's important to have books which appeal to reluctant readers and the brief easy books which can be read in a single period are worthwhile in terms of convenience and children's satisfaction'. Certainly helping them to gain confidence and a developing sense of mastery with books they can handle is the right direction here, but this department disagrees with their suggested examples taken from remedial reading schemes. The department preferred to work on their incentives about being willing to read by providing a richly diverse spread of completely satisfying stories and poems, rather than supplying them with material that was consciously written down to their level, by limiting the vocabulary and syntax. So instead of *Club 75*, *Spirals* or *Stories for Today* they went for stories like *The Bakerloo Flea* (Michael Rosen), *A Likely Place* (Paula Fox), *Poems* (Vivian Usherwood) and *Dinner ladies Don't Count* (Bernard Ashley), and decided on a special departmental policy of using lively picture story books as a part of the class library choice – stories like *Not Now Bernard* (David McKee), *How Tom Beat Captain Najork and His Hired Sportsmen* (Russell Hoban), *Dogger* (Shirley Hughes), *Come Away from the Water, Shirley* (John Burningham), *Flat Stanley* (Jeff Brown), *Hi, Cat!* (Ezra Jack Keats) and *A Walk in the Park* (Anthony Browne).

Range of style, genre and fresh narrative strategies are also worth considering in our selections if we are going to encourage children to extend their reading experiences. From the clipped, comic moral fables of James Thurber (and the darker tone of Julius Lester's fables in *The Knee-High Man*), the diary narration of *Only a Game?* (Eamon Dunphy) and *Z for Zachariah* (Robert C. O'Brien), the fractured way of telling in *Breaktime* (Aidan Chambers) and *Slake's Limbo* (Felice Holman), the attempt to fuse together a romance genre with a supernatural convention in John Gordon's stories in *The Spitfire Grave* and *Ghost on the Hill*, through to the calmer serenities of Cor Van der Heuvel's *Haiku* anthology and Roy Palmer's ballad and folk song collections, we catch something of the possible range of material available.

Sustaining interest and helping children to choose books

Keeping pupil interest in a familiar choice of books is difficult. Frequent topping up, adding to and changing of books is necessary if the children are not going to turn away from something that has become stalely predictable. But the most significant factor in all this is the potential influence of a committed teacher wanting to share enthusiasms.

An informed and lively teacher can make all the difference; drawing the pupils' attention to new stories, reminding them of old favourites, explaining what is available in the class library and book boxes, putting on book displays, creating the time for browsing and, most importantly of all, helping children at the point of choice. Many children depend too much on the book's appearance to make their choice (like the reader who said, 'I look at the covers first and see which one has a nice cover, and then I read the passage about it, and if I think it sounds good I start to read it ...') and often they need unobtrusive, sympathetic guidance from the teacher.

One of the best ways of helping children to choose is the departmental use of reading suggestions' lists (see below). Every year one English department spends a great deal of time working together, especially in the summer term, in searching for good stories to requisition and add to these lists. The lists are reprinted over the summer holiday and given out to the pupils in the first few weeks of the September term. The children fold them and Sellotape them into the back pages of their exercise books or reading journals. If they were just left there they would be worse than useless, but a real effort is made in helping the child actively to use the lists in looking for a suitable book in school or class library. Their teachers often talk through the lists, explaining what some of the stories are about, and encouraging the pupils to underline books read or possible books they might like to look out for. And the lists also help harassed teachers to remember what the fuller possibilities of book choice are at a certain age.

As a department what they are aiming for, fitfully and with only the inevitably partial success, is a heightening of independent awareness in pupils of 'book titles, series, authors, the processes involved in choosing books' so that they feel more confident in finding their own way around in the world of books.

Reading extracts to the class

One primary way of sparking off curiosities about reading and motivating pupils' interests in stories is for the teacher to read carefully chosen extracts from some of the books in the class library. Reading aloud is a neglected art. A good reader can often make the words lift off the page and enter the pupils' head with the right dramatic emphasis, timing and tone. One particular example will do – the raft building episode from Gwen Grant's '*Private – Keep out!*'

The selection of an especially riveting opening (like *Charlotte's Web*, E.B. White), incident or episode is a central aspect of the teacher's repertoire for stimulating interest. And here the Gwen Grant incident has been chosen because of its suitability for reading aloud and making an immediate impression on the pupils. Its suitability lies in the general racy comic telling, the snappy dialogue, the unusual independent girl's viewpoint and the possibilities for dramatic enactment. Here is the full extract first:

'... we all went down to the sand quarry today. All the big lads were there as well with it being a Saturday afternoon. They were all hammering and sawing and banging away at these pieces of wood they'd got from the wood-yard so I went over and says to our Joe, 'What are you doing?' and he says, 'Wouldn't you like to know?' and I says, 'Yes, that's why I'm asking', and he says, 'Mind your own business', so I went and laid on top of one of the cliffs and watched them for a bit.

They were nailing all the little pieces to the big pieces and then when they'd finished they were laying them side by side and joining them together. I could see then they were making a raft.

Anyway, when they'd got all these pieces of wood nailed together, they fetched four empty tin drums from the pile the old watchman kept near his shed and they laid the raft on top of these drums and started tying them on with rope.

Our Pete shouts to one of the lads, 'I don't think we've got enough rope to make sure these drums stop on. Shall we fetch some more just to be on the safe side?' Then all these lads go mutter, mutter, yers, yers, and so they all decide to go and see if the wood-yard man has any spare pieces of rope they can borrow. They went off and left one little lad on guard over this stupid raft they'd made.

I went down the cliff and I says to this little lad, 'Do you want a sweet?' and he says, 'Why?' and I says, 'Oh, never mind, never mind. If you don't want one, it doesn't worry me.' He stood there, and then he says, 'What kind?' and I says, 'Caramel,' and he says, 'What I got to do for it?' I says, 'Climb that cliff,' and he says, 'Cor blimey, that's nothing.' I says, 'That's what you say, but what do you do?' and he says, 'Where's the caramel first then?' and I showed it to him, my very last caramel, and he says, 'All right,' and he went running across the sand to the cliffs.

I looked down at the empty tin drums under the raft and carefully unscrewed all the caps and put them in my pocket. Then the little lad comes back and he says, 'There you are. Told you it was easy,' and I gave him the caramel and went back and laid on the cliff top again and all the lads came running into the quarry and wrapped about three hundred feet of rope round their stupid raft and I wondered if any of them would notice that none of the tin drums had their caps on. And they didn't.

I heard our Tone shout, 'Right! Ready to launch!' Boy, they certainly make me sick, thinking they're admirals or something. Then they all moved the raft into the pond and climbed on board.

Our Pete was standing there with a long bit of wood and he was paddling away as if they were in the middle of the Atlantic Ocean and then I heard our Joe shout, 'We're sinking!' and I could see all white bubbles on top of the pond from where the water was filling the empty drums and the raft was sinking lower and lower.

Our Pete was still paddling away though and he was shouting, 'Get it back to the bank! Get it back to the bank!' and all the lads started paddling with their hands. Then our stupid Tone stands up and starts saluting this little scruffy bit of a flag they had flying from a brush handle they'd stuck in the middle of the raft, just like shipwrecked sailors do on the pictures, and then our Joe stands up and salutes and then our Pete and all the other lads, one after the other. That was the last I saw of them, them standing up saluting as the raft slowly sank to the bottom of the pond. When I left, they were up to their waists already. Boys certainly are stupid. I thought I'd fall off the cliff laughing.'

The way I try to read it in the classroom goes something like this:

Passage	Reader's Interpretation
1 '... we all went down ... says to our Joe'.	1 I try and bring out the physical directness of the 'big lads'' activities by stressing '*hammering ... sawing ... banging*'.
2 'What are you doing? ... them for a bit.'	2 The tension at the heart of the extract between the girl's and the boy's perspectives comes through here in the contrasted voices. So I make the girl's voice openly and innocently inquisitive meeting the smug, know-it-all, superiority of the male replies, 'Wouldn't you like to know', etc.
3 'They were nailing ... on the safe side?'	3 Children like dramatic, 'as if you were there' sound effects so I cup my hands over my mouth and

Passage	*Reader's Interpretation*
	try and produce a distanced, echoey effect for Pete's shout, 'I don't think we've got ...'
4 'Then all these lads go ... they can borrow.'	4 I always add a few more 'mutters' and 'yers' in attempting to catch the secretive whispering of the boys.
5 'They went off ... raft they'd made.'	5 I enjoy this sentence, slowing down to emphasize each separate word that expresses the puniness of the look out, '*one/little/lad*' and then putting that against the girl's viewpoint in the accentuated 'stupid'.
6 'I went down the cliff ... running across the sand to the cliffs.'	6 The dangling the carrot exchange. One of the best parts of the extract. I try to bring out the variety of tones in this paragraph. I'll take it step by step:
(a) 'Do you want a sweet?'	(a) Innocently crafty
(b) 'Why?'	(b) Suspicious.
(c) 'Oh, never mind, never mind. If you don't want one, it doesn't worry me.'	(c) Loftily unperturbed/a seeming indifference that attracts further attention.
(d) 'He stood there, and then he says ...'.	(d) Quite a long, waiting pause after 'says'.
(e) 'What kind?'	(e) A slow, grudging question despite his better judgement.
(f) 'Caramel ... Climb that cliff.'	(f) A breathless quickening of pace. A snappy exchange.
(g) 'Cor blimey, that's nothing.'	(g) A flexing of male muscle. Swaggering. Bold. Contemptuous.
(h) 'That's what you say, but what do you do?'	(h) A skilful teasing, egging the boy on to prove himself.
(i) 'Where's the caramel first then?'	(i) Just checking it out before he plunges.
(j) 'All right.'	(j) Firm. Decisive. Steeling himself for massive difficulties.
7 'I looked down ... Told you it was easy ...'	7 The shrewd, deft actions of the girl are contrasted with the panting boastfulness of the 'little lad'. I try and produce faithful sound effects for the breathlessness. But

Passage	*Reader's Interpretation*
	it sometimes goes wrong, or the words get blurred.
8 '... and I gave him ... And they didn't'.	8 I make my voice rise in colloquial exaggeration to do justice to the empty extravagance of the boys' actions in 'wrapped about three hundred feet of rope round their stupid raft ...' and then soften my reading to point up the sly solidarity with the reader in, 'And they didn't'.
9 'I heard our Tone ... climbed on board.'	9 I do the cupping hands over mouth effect for Tone's shout and try to stress the contrast between the assertive pride of 'Ready to launch' and the girl's debunking comment.
10 'Our Pete ... sinking lower and lower.'	10 I make my voice pompous and swaggering for Pete 'paddling away as if they were in the middle of the Atlantic Ocean'. I try and surprise the listener with a terrified falsetto whine in Joe's 'We're sinking' and then slow the reading down so that the 'sinking lower and lower' seems to be trailing away.
11 'Our Pete was still paddling ... one after the other.'	11 For the first three lines of this bit I go for a fast, feverish reading with Pete sounding increasingly desperate. Then I try and sound sonorous for the pompous flourish of the boys' salute, put suddenly against a slangy, down to earth reading of the domestic details ('little scruffy bit of a flag they had flying from a brush handle they'd stuck in the middle of the raft') I try and bring out the sheep mentality of the boys by making the 'one after the other' sound flatly repetitive.
12 'That was the last ... fall off the cliff laughing.'	12 I give this final part all I've got. The first two lines deserve a serene, 'glorious, technicolour sunset ending' rendering, with my head gazing off into the far

Passage	*Reader's Interpretation*
	distance. Then a crisp change of voice at, 'When I left' bringing back reality and, finally, underlining '*boys certainly are stupid*' and a derisory hoot in the last line.

Of course it never comes out like this all at once but that is what I'm aiming for in angling for the pupils' attention and in trying to awaken their curiosity about what I'm reading.

Sharing lessons

Pupils need a chance to talk through their class library choice with their friends. If the teacher sets aside an occasional twenty-minute swap shop (in small groups of three or four) pupils can more fully possess the reading experience for themselves by having to explain it to somebody else, and, simultaneously, they can generate interest in what is available. Children seem to listen more carefully to personal recommendations from other members of the group rather than teacher suggestions from the front.

In one department a teacher organizes a regular weekly sharing session within the reading period so that working within small groups pupils take turns to tell the others about what they are reading. The usual pattern of exchange within the groups is for one person to give a detailed account of what the story is about, and then the other members to question the person more closely. These questions can become a bit of a routine but there is always the chance for expressing genuine curiosity. Here are two examples from four members of a first year group:

(A)
It's about this boy ... when he's walking home from school ... he's walking down this alleyway and he sees these young Primary school boys ... beating this ... sorta ... Norwegian type of boy up ... and they're all mocking him and

they won't give this Norwegian boy his ball back ... so this
other boy walks down this alleyway and he tells all these
little kids to get lost and go away and give the other boy his
ball back – so they do as they're told and the Norwegian
boy gets his ball back ... and ever since then ... the boy
who got his ball back ... he thinks the boy who saved him
is his hero ... and he's always following him about ... and
thinks he saved his life and everything ... so anyway this
boy follows him all over the school and everywhere ... and
the other boy gets a bit sick of him ... but he doesn't really
mind ... and between them they find out about all these
crimes ... and this Norwegian boy is in a poor family and
everything and never has much to eat ... and they find out
about this disabled man ... who's going to get killed and
everything ... and there's lots of action in it ... and there's
all sorts of people getting killed ... and they're solving all
these mysteries...

Q. Is it suitable for boys and girls?

Yea ... very suitable.

Q. Is it exciting?

Yea ... all the way through there's lots of excitement
and they are always up to something.

Q. Can you plot the end ... in the adventures? Can you
guess what's going to happen next?

Well you see it's all one adventure ... you can't really
... it's quite difficult ... there's lots of little clues but
you can't really tell what's going to happen so it's quite
good.

Q. Do you think it could happen in real life?

Well it's a bit ... at the beginning there's facts about a
crippled man ... so you have to really read it ... but I
don't think it could happen quite like that ... but it
could happen ... but not exactly like it was in the story.

Q. What people would you advise this book for … what age group?

Anything from about twelve to fourteen.

Q. So it's fairly advanced reading?

Quite … it's very good though.

(B)

Striker written by Kenneth Cope … this book's about football … it's about this lad who's ever so good about football and his father's an ex-football player but in playing football he'd broken his leg and it ruined his career … and this lad really wanted to play football but his father wouldn't let him because he didn't want him to have an injury like he had done … they never had a stable home … they kept moving about … and they stopped at this one place … and this lad saw these boys playing football so he went over to see what they were like … and they were fairly rubbish compared to his standards and they were mocking him … because he lived in a caravan and everything and they wouldn't let him play … eventually … he got a game with them … he was actually brilliant compared to them … they resented this a bit … they were a bit jealous of him … one of the team's sisters took a fancy to them … that was the boy … and the lad who was the brother of this girl … was a bit dumb you see … and everybody used to take it out on him … particularly when his sister was fancying this lad … eventually when Ben's father found out that he was playing football he told Ben off … said you can play football as long as you're careful … so he was watching him one day … and he went down and he had to be taken off from the match and his father said, 'Oh you're definitely not playing football anymore', but then Ben told him he was alright and everything so he played and his father became the manager and they went on to success and they won the League Cup and everything.

Q. Sounds a bit like football and nothing but football.

Yea but it's not all about football ... it centres around football ... it tells you what they got up to ... also they're fairly good adventures you know ... they go all over the place.

Q. So there are a lot of laughs outside the football stadium?

Yea they have a good time together playing about you know.

Q. Is it a book worth reading?

Yea if you're interested in football but you don't really care much about it ... I would advise mostly boys to read it as girls would also enjoy it as girls play a big part in it.

Q. You know his dad ... in the end does he change his mind about his son playing?

Yea at the start you get the impression that he is mean but ...

Q. But he's doing it for his own good.

At the end he really becomes interested in the team.

Q. Is there much about the actual matches?

No it's more like, 'The match was played and won by ...'

Q. What's the book called that carries on from it?

The *Striker's Second Leg*.

Q. Are there any more like that?

No it was a television series back in about 1977.

Letters to writers

Opening up conversations between pupils and writers can be one way of encouraging responsive reading. Too often children feel shut out by the print and sense that the world of books is totally distanced from their own personal worlds. Take Adrian for instance. He's a fourth former (a 15-year-old) and resistant to school in a robustly direct way. He is not just a reluctant reader. He does not see himself in the role of reader and he does not feel that stories or poems can have anything to do with the world he experiences outside school.

One day I gave him a copy of Barry Heath's vernacular poems called *M'Mam sez* produced by Your Own Stuff press, a local community publishing project. He was a bit suspicious at first but later came up at the end of a reading period and told me that he liked the book and were there any other books like that. I said that I did not think Barry had published anything more but perhaps he would like to write to him directly.

Adrian did not seem particularly bothered but over the next few days, half perfunctorily (doing what the teacher asks) and half willingly, he wrote a letter in rough, showed me and then wrote it out properly on school notepaper. Here it is:

Dear Barry,
I have read your book *M'Mam sez* and I enjoyed it very much because it's different to any normal book and it's very interesting.

To start with I found it fairly difficult because I wasn't expecting it to be like that but when I got into further depths of the book it became easier to read because I got used to the words and I could work them out easier and quicker.

I asked Mr Jackson, my English teacher if there were any more books like this one, but there wasn't. I was a bit disappointed because I would really like to read another but I can't read another if there isn't another to read so I will just have to go on and read something else instead. Usually I hate reading but I really enjoyed reading this book and that makes a change for me. The reason I liked reading it so much was because the words were wrote down just as you say them. It is best to read it aloud because you can hear yourself say the words and if you're saying them wrong you can tell and then correct yourself. One particular poem I liked was 'Cracked it' because it's short and snappy. It is also very funny in the way in which the boy walks into the shop and asked for some 'cut knackers' and then got belted around the tab by the shop keeper.

Yours sincerely
A. Hare

And Barry answered the following week:

Hello!

Thank you very much for your kind words about my book *M'Mam sez*. I'm glad you enjoyed it. It's a pleasure to know I have helped someone like you (you didn't tell me your Christian name?) and keep your eyes open, there may be another book out before long. There is going to be a TV film on Central later in the year so you'll be able to see and hear me read many other poems. Perhaps in the near future I may be able to visit your school and it would give me the greatest pleasure to meet you personally.

I would like you to know that I too hated English, reading and spelling being my worst subjects, and used to get a 'belt rahnd tab' many a time. My advice is, learn the best way you know how, don't worry about it, it'll come one day and who knows you may even end up like me and write your own book of poems!

Dialect is 'beautiful' whether it be Yorkshire, Derbyshire, Geordie or Nottinghamshire and it would be a tragedy if it were allowed to die. Why they do not teach it along with Queen's English defeats me! And remember this, writing in dialect gives you a licence to spell just how you like (crafty eh!).

Mr Jackson took a copy of another poem, 'Shopping spree' has he shown it to you? If he hasn't, tell him from me he has *got* to let you read it. AND THAT'S AN ORDER!!

I also write stories and plays, some day they may be in publication and on TV. Robin Hall, a TV Director, has shown interest and wants to work with me on a play about miners.

Well friend keep your chin up, keep reading, there's nothing finer than a good book, you're taken into another world, held spellbound by the skill of a writer and the beauty of words.

b' seein' y then weeul ay'a minit t'getha

Barry Heath

The contact with a writer who had been in the same boat as Adrian at school helps in some way to demystify the publishing process for Adrian. Books can be produced by ordinary working people, speaking in their own, authentic voices about experiences that Adrian feels close to. And, although this might not change his self-image as a reader in any permanent sense, he has at least seen that reading can have something to do with and say about his own life.

'Usually I hate reading but I really enjoyed reading this book and that makes a change for me. The reason I liked reading it so much was because the words were wrote down just as you say them.'

Writers in school

Every year at the end of the summer term in one particular school, the English department puts on Book Week in the school concert hall. It is a way of introducing the children to actual writers, making books and writers come alive in performance, giving a fresh slant on the paperbacks available in the school bookshop and class libraries, and giving some point to a tired, often fragmented, end of the school year. It's an agreed school policy now for children to be let out of any subject during the week. And the names of children going to each session are put up on the staff notice board. We try and encourage only those children with a genuine interest in taking part but there are occasional exceptions. We try and get the children to participate in the visits by reading extracts and complete stories and poems by the writers who are taking part (this year one of the writers was Nicholas Fisk so some of the short stories from *Sweets from a Stranger* were shared beforehand by teachers and pupils) and also by designing book covers and writing their own stories and poems around themes commonly used by some of the visiting writers. So that some of the sessions during Book Week can be an interaction between children reading their own stuff, the writer commenting, talking and reading, rather than the pupils sitting around like stuffed dummies.

A large, colourful banner advertising Book Week together with publishers' photographs of writers is put up on the outside of the concert hall to attract attention. Inside, the school bookshop, working with the English department, has arranged special book displays on the work of each visiting writer. There are four or five parent helpers, who work in the bookshop during the week, selling books from an extensive range of paperbacks set out on trestle tables. The pupils' book covers, stories and poems are exhibited on display screens and mounted on striking backing paper. A detailed programme is given out to every child and member of staff in the school.

So just to give you something of the flavour of the actual visit here is a brief snapshot from Michael Rosen's visit to the school during Book Week. One hundred and twenty children are stretched around him in a semi-circle. Children from some of the feeder Primary schools are sprawled out on the reading room cushions within the semi-circle.

Mike immediately relaxes the audience with, 'I know someone who can lick the bottom of their chin', swivelling his eyes and wiggling his tongue towards the bottom of his chin. 'Can you do that?' Stretched tongues. Giggles. Groans.

And then the anecdote about how he chipped one of his

teeth. He invites the pupils' own stories and then plunges into
his go-kart story/poem.

Me and my mate Harrybo
we once made a go-kart.
Everyone was making go-karts
so we had to make one.
Big Tony's was terrific
Big Tony was terrific
because Big Tony told us he was.
What he said was,
'I am TERRIFIC'
and because Big Tony was VERY big
no one said,
'Big Tony.
You are NOT terrific.'
So,
Big Tony was terrific
and Big Tony's go-kart was terrific.
And that was that.

Mike stands up to tell it, pausing for emphasis before each
'terrific'. He pronounces it 'ter-*rif*-ic'. A few laughs. Most of
the audience don't quite know what to make of it.

When Big Tony sat on his go-kart
he looked like a real driver.
He had control.
When he came down a road round our way
called Moss Lane
he could make the wind blow his hair,
pheeeeeeooooooooooph,
he could make the wheels of his go-kart go
prrrrrrrrrrrrrrrrrr
and he went
eeeeeeeeeeeeooowwwwwww
as he went past.

Using his whole body and imitating the sounds with his voice
he mimes out,

'pheeeeeeooooooooooph'
'prrrrrrrrrrrrrrrrr'

and his eyes sweep right round from right to left, eyeballs
bulging, when he mimes out, 'eeeeeeeeeeeeooowwwwwww'.
The pupils are with him now.

I was jealous of Big Tony.
I was afraid that I thought
he might be
terrific.

So me and Harrybo
we made a go-kart
out of his old pram
and some boxes and crates
we got from the off-licence.
We nailed it up with bent nails
but Harrybo's dad said,
'No no no no no
You should use big metal staples'
And he gave us some.
He said they were
'Heavy Duty'.

Heavy duty
Wow
That sounded
terrific.

Mike pauses at 'Heavy Duty', looking up with astonishment.
'Wow'!

So then we tied cord round the front cross-piece.
But Harrybo's dad said,
'No no no no no,

you should use the pram handle'
and he helped us fix
the pram handle to the cross-piece.
He said 'That'll give you
Control'
Control
Wow
That sounded
terrific.
Harrybo sat on the beer-crate
and steered,
I kneeled behind
But Harrybo's dad said
'No no no no no
you should kneel on foam pads'.
And he cut these two foam pads
for me to kneel on.
Harrybo's dad said,
'That'll help you
Last The Course.'

Last the course,
wow
That sounded
terrific.

Our go-kart was ready.
So we took it up to the top of Moss Lane
and Harrybo said,
'I'll steer', and he did.
It was fan
tastic.
It felt just like Big Tony looked.
The hair in the wind
pheeeeeeeeooooooooooooph
the wheels
prrrrrrrrrrrrrrrrr

and so we both went
eeeeeeeeeeeeeooooowwwwwwwww
So we took it up to the top
of Moss Lane again
and Harrybo said
'I'll steer',
and he did.
It was a
mazing.
The road went blurry

The hair in the wind
pheeeeeeeeoooooooph
the wheels went
prrrrrrrrrrrrrrrrr
so we both went
eeeeeeeeeooooowwwww.

The children were now waiting, eager with anticipation, for
every repeated 'terrific' and 'eeeeeeeeeooooowwwww'.

So we took it up to the top of Moss Lane again
and Harrybo said
'I'll steer,'
so I said,
'Can I have a go?'
Harrybo said,
'NO'
'Go on,' I said.
'No', he said, 'You've never done it.'
'Go on, Harrybo. Let me have a go.
Go on. I mean. Blimey.
Come on Harrybo. Go on.'
'No'.
'Oh go on. Go on. Go on.'

Mike was jumping up and down now, looking as if he wanted
to go to the toilet, with every whining, 'Go on'. All the

children recognized that, especially the Primary school ones.

'Alright' he said.
'Look out won't you.'
'Yeah yeah yeah. *I* know.' I said.
I thought,
'I'm going to be
terrific.'
My hair – pheeeoooph
wheels – prrrrrrr
me – eeeow

And away we went.
Hair – yeah – pheeeeeeeoooph
wheels – yeah – prrrrrrrrrr
me – yeah – eeeeeeeoooooow
BUT
halfway down Moss Lane
there's Moss Close
and that's where the road curves
and that's where Big Tony steers
Big Tony leans
Big Tony controls
prrrrrrrrrr
eeeeeeeoooowwww
I saw Moss Close coming up really fast
'Steer,' shouts Harrybo. 'Steer'
and I yanked on the pram handle
'uh'
and the whole world
went round once and twice
and three times
and my head went rolling
down the road
pulling me after it
and the go-kart came for the ride
over and over and over

until my nose and my chin
and my two front teeth landed up
in the grit of the gutter.

The approaching panic on Mike's face, the dizzying whirl
in his voice and groggy expression, and the 'two front teeth
(landing) up in the grit of the gutter' had the audience silent,
hushed.

Harrybo was crying.
'Wo wo wo oooo wo wo ooo'
I breathed in and it whistled.
'Whew'
'Whew'
There it was again.
I stuck my finger up to my tooth
and it was chipped.
Harrybo said,
'Your chin's bleeding'
and I said,
'Your chin's bleeding an all.'
'I know ooooooo' he said.

And then the explosive release at the climax of the story
with Harrybo crying, with Mike screwing up his face,
clenching up his eyes and wailing like a baby. The audience
just collapsed in laughter, some with tears in their eyes.

We walked home.
He pulled the kart,
got to his place
he didn't say anything.
Nothing at all.
Not a word
And he went in.
I walked on to my place
'Whew – whew – whew'
it was still whistling.

When I got in
I told mum everything
and she said, well, she said all kinds of things –
like 'Well – your teeth'll
probably fall out, you know.'
One of those nice things
that mums say.

Next day at school
they were all asking about the crash
they all looked at my tooth
and they all wanted to see the go-kart.
Harrybo said,
'You can't,
cos my dad's
chopped it up!

Chopped up.
wow
that sounded
terrible.

Hey,
when Harrybo got his racer,
his brand new racing bike for Christmas
I didn't ask him for a go on it.
I didn't.
no
I didn't.

I wonder why.

The story came to an end in a quietly subdued way, except
for the giggles at the deliberate disappointment of the
anticipation in 'terrible'. The applause flooded the whole of
the concert hall. We sold out of the Mike Rosen paperbacks
that afternoon.

Other ideas

WRITERS IN SCHOOL SCHEME

The Writers in Schools scheme was set up by the Arts Council in 1969 'to provide opportunities for educational establishments to arrange subsidized visits by creative writers'. Since 1980 the scheme has been taken over and operated by the Regional Arts Association in England, whose address can be obtained from the Arts Council (Arts Council of Great Britain, 105 Piccadilly, London W1V 0AU). The Regional Associations can provide lists of writers who are prepared to visit schools to talk about their work. Similar schemes are available in Scotland and Wales and lists may be obtained from The Scottish Arts Council, 19 Charlotte Square, Edinburgh EH2 4DF, and the Welsh Arts Council, Holst House, 9 Museum Place, Cardiff CF1 3NX. A very helpful, step by step approach to 'Inviting a writer' can be found in *Children, Language and Literature* (Milton Keynes, Open University Department of Continuing Education, 1982), p. 141.

WRITER IN RESIDENCE

Often the Regional Arts Associations can be helpful in organizing a more sustained series of visits from a writer, or a termly writer in residence scheme. (See 'Writers in School' – Stephen Eyers and Mike Rosen's account of being writers in residence at Vauxhall Manor School from *Becoming Our Own Experts* – The Talk Workshop Group, ILEA English Centre, Sutherland Street, London SW1, for classroom accounts of working the scheme.)

THE POETRY SECRETARIAT

The Poetry Society (National Poetry Centre, 21 Earls Court Square, London SW5) also helps to subsidize and organize school visits from poets. A list of writers and practical details are available on application.

ARVON FOUNDATION

The Foundation was set up 'to provide the opportunity to live and work informally with professional writers'. It runs five-day courses on fiction, poetry, television, writing, etc., and will also arrange courses for specific groups, such as schools, colleges and LEAs. Further details can be obtained from Lumb Bank, Hebden Bridge, West Yorkshire HX7 6DF, and Totleigh Barton, Sheepwash, Beaworthy, Devon EX21 5NS.

RUNNING A SCHOOL BOOKSHOP

There have been so many detailed accounts of how to set about running a school bookshop that it would be redundant to add yet another one. Here's a list of some of the best advice:

(a) A stage-by-stage introduction to running a school bookshop is to be found in 'School bookshop: You are thinking of starting a school bookshop', in *Children, Language and Literature* (Milton Keynes, Open University Department of Continuing Education, 1982), p. 141.

(b) Peter Kennerley, *Running a School Bookshop* (London, Ward Lock Educational, 1978).

(c) Deirdre Noyes, 'Running a school bookshop', in *Children, Language and Literature* (details as above).

(d) R. Hill and P. Triggs, *How to Set Up and Run a School Bookshop* (London, School Bookshop Association, 1981 – see below).

The School Bookshop Association (SBA), National Book League, Book House, 45 East Hill, Wandsworth, London SW18 2QZ, encourages the setting up of school bookshops through detailed advice and guidance. An enquiry would be well worth the effort.

Notes

1 See 'Anecdote as a content area in English' section of 'Dignifying anecdote', from *English in Education*, Spring 1983.

2 See Donald Fry, 'Reflecting on English: keeping work diaries', in Mike Torbe (ed.), *Language, Teaching and Learning*, vol. 3: *English*, London, Ward Lock Educational, 1981.

3 J. Ingham, *Books and Reading Development – The Bradford Book Flood Experiment*, London, Heinemann Educational, 1981.

5

FRESH WAYS OF
WORKING WITH TEXTS

What other things can be done with a book in the English classroom rather than just the teacher reading to the class? That is one of the questions that keeps on cropping up. But with Geoff Fox's[1] inventive lists of possibilities now readily available, detailed classroom descriptions of alternative ways of working are gradually beginning to emerge.

Instead of repeating the idea of an extensive list I want to concentrate on some of the most valuable activities in the classroom that promote pupils' *active, questioning engagement with the text*; and also to flesh out a limited number of the suggested activities with examples from the pupils' responses.

Improvising into a text

I introduced a group of fourth years to Liz Lochhead's 'Poem for my sister' from her collection, *The Grimm Sisters*. First I read the poem to them and then I asked them to read it by themselves.

Poem for my sister

My little sister likes to try my shoes,
to strut in them,
admire her spindle-thin twelve-year-old legs
in this season's styles.
She says they fit her perfectly,
but wobbles
on their high heels, they're
hard to balance.

I like to watch my little sister
playing hopscotch, admire the neat hops-and-skips of her,
their quick peck,
never-missing their mark, not
over-stepping the line.
She is competent at peever.

I try to warn my little sister
about unsuitable shoes,
point out my own distorted feet, the callouses,
odd patches of hard skin.
I should not like to see her
in my shoes.
I wish she could stay
sure footed,
    sensibly shod.

Then, dividing the group up into twos (with one three left over), I asked them to act out a conversation between big sister and little sister based on their understanding of the two girls from reading the poem, in one of the following situations:

(a) preparing for a disco
(b) sharing a bedroom
(c) shopping for clothes on a Saturday
(d) Sunday night at home getting ready for school on Monday.

The room was already arranged in a rectangular box shape so it did not take too much time to push the stackable tables back a bit and get on with it. They worked on these improvised conversations for the next twenty-five minutes with me moving around amongst the groups suggesting, listening, praising, chivvying.

A quarter of an hour before the end of the lesson (hour-length periods) I brought the pairs back into the whole group and we shared, five small groups presenting their work to the rest of the class. I just had time to set the homework:

'In play form, write out your conversation between big sister and little sister. You can invent further details but base them on an understanding of how the two girls would act from a reading of the poem.' (They had copies of the poem to take home with them.)

Here is one example from what came back.

Preparing for a disco

Little sis. Hey Jane, can I wear your red shoes tonight.

Big sis. Oh Anne, you know you can't walk in them. Anyway they look ridiculous.

Little sis. Well you wear them, and I've been practising walking in them all day. I don't wobble anymore!

Big sis. You'll be crippled by the end of the night. And how are you going to dance in them?

Little sis. I'll take them off to dance.

Big sis. Oh yeah, get them stolen or lost.

Little sis. Don't be stupid, who would pinch them?

Big sis. You're not going to wear them, they're too old for you, just like that make-up. It makes your eyes look like coal pits.

Little sis. I did it the same as yours.

Big sis. Look, why don't you wear that pretty dress and sandals, they would be more practical and ...

Little sis. Practical, I don't want to be practical! Won't you never let me grow-up. You wore make-up and high heels at my age, why can't I? You are always wanting me to look like a little baby.

Big sis. I just don't want you to make the same mistake I did. Don't wish your life away, stay young and pure. Don't turn out like me.

Little sis. But I want to be like you.

Big sis. No! Oh God you don't understand!

Little sis. I do, I understand! You want me to wear frilly dresses and sandals all my life. You're just like Mother, so protective. I'm the darling little girl who does everything right. I'm twelve almost thirteen, not a baby any more and you don't understand that, do you?

Big sis. Wear the damn shoes if you have too, cripple yourself, ruin your feet, but don't come running to me. One day you will realise, and regret it.

Designing a book cover that expresses the meaning and spirit of the book for you (including title and writer's name on the front, and a suitable blurb on the back cover)

It is sometimes difficult to persuade the pupils not to indulge in empty decoration that's got nothing to do with their interpretations of the book. But if they are encouraged to talk through the connection between their designs and their responses to the book in the process of illustrating it they can frequently become more precisely articulate in explaining the book to themselves and others. This kind of explicit commentary can also be usefully attempted in an accompanying piece of writing that is put up on display along with the finished design. Here are some examples from pupil/teacher conversations about the processes of deciding on a book cover for *Nancekuke* (John Branfield).

[*Nancekuke* is about Helen Roberts, whose family are forced to move from their large, old home in the Cornish countryside to a small house on a council estate because

Helen's father has died and left her mother with little more than a widow's pension. The circumstances of his death seem peculiar to Helen. He had worked at Nancekuke, a chemical defence experimental establishment, and just before his death had been doing research on a German nerve gas bomb; he had died of leukaemia. Helen cares desperately that there should be an investigation into her father's death, but her mother is emotionally opposed to the idea. So Helen conducts her own defiant investigation into the affair, helped by a journalist her father had known, and Mike, a sixth-former at a nearby school who is in love with her. Helen in time comes to terms with her father's death and the cause of it.]

Deciding on a book cover for *Nancekuke*

Ian ... the book is generally about chemical warfare so I think ... the design for the cover should have the plant in the back ... with smoke coming out of the chimneys and things ... it should look pretty sinister with barbed wire all round it ... um ... no windows at all ... like Dave says ... I think the barbed wire should come out into the foreground as well ... um ... I put the two faces either side of the chemical warfare plant ... because it signifies the chemical warfare coming between the relationship ... between Mike and Helen ... um ... the signs at the front ... er ... you know 'Keep Out' signs all signifies the danger of the plant ... I think we should put a few dead seals here and there ...

Chris I think also we could have some guards on the gates ... you know a pair of gates ... lorries can get in and pick stuff up ... we really ought to have some guards on the gates really because ... you know ... it's such an important place ... you would tend to have guards on it ... and that would make it really ... look more sinister

David ... and cameras looking out ... on the building ... look out on the ... want to know what's happening ... they've got those video things ...

Teacher Why would they be doing that?

Ian I think they should have guard dogs on it ... pictures of guard dogs instead of guards ... they look more sinister with fangs ... and drooling teeth ... and dribbling all over ...

*   *   *   *

Teacher Why don't Bill, Helen and Mike appear in your drawing?

Chris Well really the main story's around ... the station

Kerry Yea ... it's more to do with chemicals ... and the pollution ...

David But it's between that boy and girl ... isn't it?

Martin It's probably more about those two people ... than it is about chemical warfare ... you ought to have Helen and Mike more into the picture than the chemical plant ...

Teacher Where would you put them?

David Put them in front ... not with it ... make it so ... she's not bothered about ... she's more bothered about him ... so they're both talking to each other ...

Paul I'd rather put the faces at the side really ... because I think the chemical plant ... brings them two together ... really ... and not have Bill Wyatt in the picture at all ... because he's sort of forgotten ... out of Helen's mind really ...

Kerry I think you ought to put more people as well ... more people who are involved ...

Teacher Who else might you put in?

Paul The mother

Kerry Fishermen

Ian Helen's sister

Teacher What have they got to do with it?

    Ian They're part of a basic family relationship ... they influence her, don't they? Cause they're her family ... influence her decisions ...

       *   *   *   *

Teacher What have you done with yours, Paul?

    Paul I've shown barbed wire, sign saying 'Keep Out' ... you know to make everybody stay out the way ... black smoke coming out of the chimney to show pollution and that ... and I decided instead of putting 'Nancekuke' the title and author of the book on the spine ... I decided to do it in a sign ... to make it blend in with the background ... that's better than spoiling the design of the cover really

Teacher D'you think people are put off by covers?

    David If you get a good cover ... people are going to ... see what it's like ... if it's a good cover ...

    Chris If you see a good cover that looks interesting they would tend to read the book ... whereas if it wasn't a very good cover at all ... they would think it was a load of rubbish ... it's not even worth picking up ...

    Paul In a way the cover's got to tell the story of the book in a sort of picture form really ...

Deciding how to read aloud a poem/extract/story to another group

Getting on the inside of a writer's intentions is another important way of making a reading experience your own.[2] The activity of deciding how to read aloud a text can often encourage this process.

I divided a second-year group into small groups of three and four, gave them each a different poem or short story, or they had the chance to choose one by themselves, and told them I would like them to decide how to read the text aloud to the rest of the class in a whole group. They had an hour to organize themselves and prepare themselves for the reading. The following English period was totally given over to a small group exchange. I want to focus on the way one group tackled Roger McGough's 'First day at school'. First the poem from *In the Classroom*, and then a transcript with the teacher finding out how they're getting on:

> *First day at school*
> A millionbillionwillion miles from home
> Waiting for the bell to go. (To go where?)
> Why are they all so big, other children?
> So Noisy? So much at home they
> must have been born in uniform
> Lived all their lives in playgrounds
> Spent the years inventing games
> that don't let me in. Games
> that are rough, that swallow you up.
>
> And the railings.
> All around, the railings.
> Are they to keep out wolves and monsters?
> Things that carry off and eat children?
> Things you don't take sweets from?
> Perhaps they're to stop us getting out
> Running away from the lessins. Lessin.
> What does a lessin look like?
> Sounds small and slimy.
> They keep them in glassrooms.
> Whole rooms made out of glass. Imagine.
>
> I wish I could remember my name
> Mummy said it would come in useful.
> Like wellies. When there's puddles.
> Yellowwellies. I wish she was here.
> I think my name is sewn on somewhere

Perhaps the teacher will read it for me.
Tea-cher. The one who makes the tea.

T. How do you think it ought to be done?
R. You ought to sound ... um ... a bit bewildered ...
C. Slowly ...
T. Why do you think that?
I. Because he's asking so many questions about why they're all so big ... and so noisy ... I don't think he's been to a school yet ...
R. He's just moved or something ...
M. And he doesn't know who the people are because he's just started ...
R. He thinks they're all used to going to school ... they're just the same really but they know the other people which they've gone with ...
C. They've got friends ... or maybe he's felt shy ... and other people are going round in gangs ...
T. So do you think you'd read it in a bewildered voice?
J. Um ...
R. He can't have been to any other school because he's asking ... asking about the bell to go ... to go where ... and about the teacher ... the one who makes the tea ... because he doesn't know what anyone's doing ...
T. So how does this show a little boy's difficulties on his first day in a strange school?
C. He doesn't know what to expect ... and doesn't know where to go ...
T. Would you read it in a slow or fast voice?
J. Slow.
T. Why?
C. Because he doesn't know anything ... if you read it in a fast voice you'd feel as if he knows it ...
T. What about the railings bit?
M. He's sort of locked in ...
I. Doesn't know what a lesson is ...

C. He doesn't know what it's all about...

M. He thinks the railings are to keep monsters off...

T. Why might he think of monsters there then?

I. Because little children have a vivid imagination...

M. Because where he went before ... where he used to live it was all right ... and he knew everything but here it could be different ... and perhaps he never saw school railings before ... and it's all different...

J. It might be an old school or something ... not a new modern one and he's used to seeing this old house ... sort of...

T. What other things did you find strange in starting at a new school?

J. People's names...

C. When they gave you a bottle of milk ... and if you didn't like it they made you drink it ... they did me...

M. I wasn't allowed out dinner times (voices obscure each other).

R. The dinner ladies used to stand over you and you didn't know why they were ... because at home if you just wanted to leave ... something they kind of didn't mind ... but there they did...

C. Yea ... they used to shout at ... if you ate slowly they used to hurry you up...

T. What things did you misunderstand?

C. Before I went to school I had a morning in there ... and I couldn't understand that why everybody else ... the people I'd made friends with weren't there when I came ... because they'd gone up ... and I couldn't understand why...

T. 'I wish I could remember my name
   Mummy said it would come in useful.'
   How would you read that?

I. Sort of slow ... trying to remember what ... what your name is...

R. Why can't he remember his name?

C. He's kind of shy or something ... he's worried about it ...

(Here we listen to one member of the group reading the complete poem aloud to the rest of the group.)

T. What do you think of Dawn's reading?

M. She read it well but not softly enough or explaining ... she didn't get the sort of lost tone in ...

C. I thought she had ... but she read a bit too fast all the way through ...

R. She got it at the beginning ... but it's just a little bit when she says 'Tea – cher' ... she read it a bit too happily ...

C. It shouldn't have been read like that ... it sounds as if she's calling him ...

T. How should it? ...

I. ... confusingly ...

J. Yea ... he's thinking about the one who makes the tea ...

C. He's thinking it over in his head ...

T. So he's not being cheeky?

C. No.

(Here we listen to a tape cassette reading by Roger McGough of his own poem.)

J. He said the 'Tea – cher' quietly ...

C. Yea I like that ...

T. Why?

R. It was like he was thinking it ... he was kind of turning it over in his mind ... saying it ...

C. He wasn't calling people ... he was just mentioning it ...

I. I got the feeling he was reading it a little bit fast ...

J. Parts of it ...

I. Yea ... when he was asked ... when he's asking questions ...

Arguing and thinking about what you read through diagrams

Translating and re-organizing their thoughts into another medium often produces a valuable distancing effect that helps pupils to pull together miscellaneous reactions into more coherent patterns of meaning. As a fifth-form pupil remarked, 'It helped you sort out in your mind who was with who, and who wasn't.'

See the detailed examples of this approach in the case study section below, 'Dealing with a set book in literature at 16+'.

Keeping a reading log or journal to act as a running commentary on what you read

Stopping every two or three chapters, or when the pupil feels she wants to, use the reading log/journal to record fleeting first impressions caught on the wing, e.g. questions, thoughts, blockages, personal experiences that connect with the text, excitements, illustrations, summaries of small group talk, arguments, moments when the point of the book becomes clear, cover designs, conversations with the teacher, creative writing on aspects of the book, etc.

For a working example of this approach see 'Meeting Books: talking and writing about literature' by David Jackson from Mike Torbe (ed.), *Language, Teaching and Learning*, vol. 3: *English* (London, Ward Lock Educational, 1981).

Visual interrogation (collage work)

A difficult approach to handle first time, so don't hope for instant results. But some of the work can be unusual and can offer more open modes of response that seem to suit some pupils. It requires careful preparation (e.g. a plentiful supply of scissors, Sellotape, black sugar-paper, magazines to cut up, ordinary drawing paper, a wide selection of scraps of material, etc.).

To start off I gave each member of this fourth-year group a copy of a poem I had just discovered called 'Prince Kano' by Edward Lowbury:

Prince Kano

In a dark wood Prince Kano lost his way
And searched in vain through the long summer's day.
At last, when night was near, he came in sight
Of a small clearing filled with yellow light,
And there, bending beside his brazier, stood
A charcoal burner wearing a black hood.
The Prince cried out for joy: 'Good friend, I'll give
What you will ask: guide me to where I live.'
The man pulled back his hood: he had no face –
Where it should be there was an empty space.

Half dead with fear the Prince staggered away,
Rushed blindly through the wood till break of day;
And then he saw a larger clearing, filled
With houses, people; but his soul was chilled,
He looked around for comfort, and his search
Led him inside a small, half-empty church
Where monks prayed 'Father,' to one he said,
'I've seen a dreadful thing; I am afraid.'
'What did you see, my son?' 'I saw a man
Whose face was like ...' and, as the Prince began,
The monk drew back his hood and seemed to hiss,
Pointing to where his face should be, 'Like this?'

I then gave the group the following, step by step, instructions.

(a) Make sense of the poem 'Prince Kano' by Edward Lowbury, through a visual exploration.
(b) You can work by yourself or in small groups.
(c) Don't rush into it! Give yourself time to re-read the poem several times, think about it, make rough notes on how you can understand the poem by putting it into picture form. Talk it through in small groups if you like.

(d) Together or by yourself select details, lines (or go for a whole feeling or atmosphere) that you think ought to be included in your visual.

(e) Think carefully about the right kind of visual for what you want to do, e.g. your own drawing, collage, strip cartoon, etc.

(f) A collage means arranging different pieces of pictures and materials together on a sugar-paper background so that the whole picture makes sense, in your own way, of the poem that you've just read. Here are some examples of the kinds of things you can stick on to a collage: coloured wools, tissue paper, cellophane, buttons, found objects, scraps of material, cut out photographs from magazines, your own drawing, cut out silhouettes etc.

Figure 3 *Prince Kano*: visual interrogation by Louise Burgess

Figure 4 *Prince Kano*: visual interrogation by Tim Bean

(g) Write a short description (to go alongside your visual) that explains how you were trying to make sense of the poem through the way you did your visual.

This is what the group came up with. Three written explanations and some visuals (Figures 3–5):

I took all this as a man lost and confused and couldn't understand why. There were people all around him who should help and wouldn't. The drawing helped me decide all this. I saw the man of splendour first, but then it was him who is in the dark, lost world and not people below him. So my drawing turned into darkness, and the obvious person for help, the preacher of the church wouldn't give it. I see the prince as a lost and lonely man deprived in life with no

Figure 5   *Prince Kano*: a collage

friends, no kindliness given to him. I think the poem's message is not to take everything for granted. (JACQUI SMITH)

My Prince Kano visual is designed to show both the story and the evilness it is built upon. The centre picture is supposed to show evil things, or scary things and the outer one's various scenes from the poem. The prince shows a feeling from happiness to terror twice in the poem (finding the burner and seeing no face and finding the church and seeing no face to a priest.) It is a long summer day (perhaps midsummer) on which bad things might happen, especially in a deep, dark wood. He thinks he can find a friend to help him but instead finds evil. Perhaps the prince would have ignored both burner and priest had he not been in need of help and this may be why evil appears to him? (TIM BEAN)

The prince seems to be experiencing something which is absolutely new to him – fear. Being happy before, where he had all he wanted, then getting lost and finding terror. Something he isn't familiar with and not knowing what's going to happen to him. He wants to go home to love, not be lost in a place he doesn't know about, a place that's dark and evil. (LOUISE BURGESS)

For me it is a valid justification for trying out this method for Jacqui to comment: 'The drawing helped me decide all this'.

Anecdotalizing into the text

Anecdote can be a significant, thinking tool about what they read for many children. See the detailed examples in both spoken and written forms included in the case study below, 'Homing in to *The Battle of Bubble and Squeak*, (Philippa Pearce) through personal anecdotes'.

Answering in role

This tactic often helps pupils to engage more closely with the text, and proves a useful way of encouraging them to try out somebody else's perceptions. In attempting to remain consistent it frequently takes them back to the text.

I was investigating a radio script called *Julian* by Ray Jenkins with a group of 13-year-olds. (The play takes place in an empty, abandoned church and centres on a dare contest for the leadership of a gang between a supposed softy, called Julian, and the present leader, called Finch, who is insecure and apparently hard-boiled. Julian wins the dare and takes over the gang by ruthlessly being prepared to break the church's stained glass windows placed there in honour of those soldiers who were killed in the two world wars, while Finch is unable to carry out Julian's dare for him – killing a baby tortoise.) Wanting them to penetrate deeper into the subtleties of the text I asked them to divide a page of their English exercise books into two and to make fully developed notes, with points accompanying precise examples, about the different qualities of each person, Julian and Finch.

I explained why I had asked them to do this, telling them that on the following day in the open space of the House area we would be breaking up into twos and threes and taking it in turns to put ourselves into the position of either Julian or Finch. They would then be questioned about their actions and behaviour by the other members of the group as if they really were those characters. Using their notes I wanted them to answer these queries in role and to try and imagine what Finch and Julian would be thinking and feeling at any given moment throughout the play.

Here is just one quick example, from Samantha being questioned as Finch, the fallen leader:

Samantha as Finch

Why did you choose the church?

S. Because it was a quiet place and nobody else could see – nobody could come and interrupt us...

To see what?

S. A fight.

Were you going to get him?

S. There was going to be...

Why did you want to fight him?

S. Because he was getting on my nerves ... he was about to take the gang off me...

How d'you work that out?

S. Because he was only thinking ... he was really big ... making a big head of himself ... everybody was suddenly beginning to like him ... so I thought I better do something about it.

Did you trust your friends? [laughter]

S. Yea but he might have put them off me.

... did it worry you that you might not be the leader of the gang?

S. Yea ... because it was sort of ... my pride ... sort of thing...

Important to you...

S. Yea.

Haven't you got any other friends then?

S. Yea course I have...

Why are you bothered then ... I wouldn't be bothered...

S. Because they were my best friends.

Why can't you just share a gang?

S. Because I don't like him ... he's one of my enemies.

Why don't you all go together?

S. You've just asked that.

Why didn't you kill the tortoise? ... to prove that you were a big head?

S. Doesn't mean to prove that I'm a big head...

Alright then ... to prove that you were the best?

S. Because I'm not going to go round killing live things ... just for that...

Well Julian would have done...

S. I know he would have done ... because he doesn't care...

Well! leaders probably don't care ... they're not meant to care...

S. Yes they are.

Detective work: group prediction methods with complete stories that make you want to read on

For examples of an attempt to motivate adequately group prediction work by absorbing it into the main bloodstream of reading see the case study below, 'Learning to become an active reader' (using prediction approaches to *The Turbulent Term of Tyke Tiler* by Gene Kemp).

Alternative openings and endings in short stories

A proper appreciation of why a writer uses a particular ending or opening to a story usually moves the reader on to a deeper, structural sense of the whole, linked network of meaning in the story. As Margaret Meek remarks in *Learning to read* (London, Bodley Head, 1982): '[the reader] understands how the ending [of a story] helps him to reconstrue the beginning'. So re-working possible openings and endings can prompt pupils into searching for more coherent connections between the separate units of the story.

Working with a group of 15-year-olds on Hemingway's short story 'The end of something'[3] I set them the following assignment:

> Basing your ideas on a close reading of the story (and bringing in the same characters and plot) write one possible alternative opening *and* one possible alternative ending. Also write a commentary on both opening and ending, giving your reasons for writing them like that as clearly and as thoughtfully as you can.

(A) *Pupils' responses*

Opening
'We'll be passing the old mill soon', he thought. 'I hope it doesn't remind her too much, of all the good times. That will make it all the more hard.' Nick sat rowing, deep in thought as Marjorie faced him in silence.

'She knows', he thought, 'she must do by now. There's no way out now.'

'There's the Mill, look Nick', Marjorie said. 'We used to go there so often in the early days, after it closed.'

The Mill used to be the nucleus of the town. If there was no Mill, there would be no Hortons Bay. Things had changed since then though. Since it had closed down, the empty yards and buildings had become the haunt of couples such as Nick and Marjorie who wanted to get to know each other better.

'Haven't been there lately have we Nick? Why, what's going wrong?'

Nick rowed on in silence. Not bothering to reply.

'Why don't I answer her?', he thought. 'Get it over with once and for all. Then it would be finishcd.'

They rowed on out of sight of the Mill following the shoreline...

Commentary

I think that the original opening written by Hemingway, talks too much about the history of the Mill. It could be shortened quite a lot but I don't think however that it should be missed out altogether. This is because it provides an important link with the couple's past and present, and the same that happened to the Mill is happening to them: The most important thing to one person was the other. Their relationship was strong and powerful, but then something went wrong and it began to get worse. Now it is obvious that it is going to end. There is a lot going through Nick's mind as he rows along in the boat. He is trying to sort everything out and find a way to tell Marjorie without upsetting her too much. Meanwhile Marjorie senses that something is wrong, and has a good idea what it is, but is afraid to face up to it. She uses the Mill and its memories to try and get Nick to tell her what he is thinking, she knows he is keeping something from her.

Ending

As they sat on the blanket in silence Marjorie made the decision – 'If he's not going to tell me off his own back I'll make him.'

'Nick it's over isn't it, you don't want to see me anymore.' He turned away from her to hide his face, ashamed to look at her.

'Yes, Marjorie it is, I'm sorry but it isn't working out any more is it?'

There was a pause as Marjorie took in what Nick had said. 'Isn't working he says, but it could do, it could be as great as it was before.'

'We could try again', Nick said. 'But it wouldn't work I know it. None of it's your fault though it's all mine.'

'Is there someone else?'

'No, not as such but . . .'.

'Goodbye Nick!' Marjorie got up, walked down the beach and began to pull the boat out of the trees to join Nick.

Commentary

Marjorie is filled with hate for Nick. she despises him because he is bringing an end to their relationship. But deep down she really cares about him and regrets that she can't do anything to win him back. Her hate is shown in her first decision of my ending, and then her true feelings show through when she thinks that it could be as good as before.

Nick is disgusted at himself, for having to finish with Marjorie under these circumstances and wishes that it could be different. He wants to tell her the real reason and is about to tell her but doesn't carry it out.

When she turned to see Bill, she realized the real truth.

(SARAH PRICE)

(B)

Opening

It was almost three weeks since Marjorie experienced the first fishing with Nick and the journeys out onto the lake now became a routine in hers and Nick's relationship. It was a routine she loved to fulfil and take part in. But today it was different, something was the matter with Nick, he seemed faraway from her, she wanted to reach out and love him close to her face, but there was something inside her stopped her doing so. She tried not to let him know that she sensed something was wrong, maybe he was just feeling down after yesterday, surely he would get used to not having Bill around.

Marjorie sat in the front of the boat as she always did, facing Nick. She liked to watch him.

Nick was quiet, she tried to make conversation, his replies were short lived and unenthusiastic, she tried to talk as much as usual, not knowing what difference it would make. All the time Marjorie was pushing one thought to the back of her mind, but she wasn't sure what it was, probably because she didn't want to.

Commentary

I tried to write the beginning about Marjorie's feelings, her side of the story. I did the same with the ending but I found it much harder. It was difficult to understand what she was feeling when she rowed away in the boat. Did she hate him? Or love him even more? Or couldn't she understand herself? What her feelings were?

(KATE GISBY)

(C)

Opening

'You lost', laughed Bill.

'What you going to make me do then', asked Nick dejectedly.

'I dare you to chuck your girlfriend.'
'I c... can't, y... you can't...'.
'You can't back out now. I'll name the place and the time all right.'
'I suppose so.'
'O.K., the old ruin, at dusk, you can be doing some fishing.'

Commentary
I made the alternative beginning with the dare. Also the fact that Bill knew where Nick was, and also that Nick wasn't surprised to see him. It says that he (Nick) lay there while he heard Bill come into the clearing ... how did Nick know it was Bill it could have been anyone. This enforced my theory about it being a dare.

(VERONICA RAY)

Notes

1   '24 things to do with a book', '36 things to do with a poem', collected in *Children, Language and Literature*, Milton Keynes, Open University Department of Continuing Education, 1982.

2   See John Branfield's comments on reading a fourth-former's journal impressions after she had read his book *Nancekuke* – 'the entries in Kim's journal are like the thoughts that go through a writer's mind' – included in 'First encounters: the importance of initial responses to literature', in *Children, Language and Literature*, ibid.

3   The story 'The end of something' is to be found in *The Snows of Kilimanjaro*; also in David Jackson, *Continuity in Secondary English* (London, Methuen, 1982, pp. 123–42) where there is a further discussion on the nature of understanding stories.

PART TWO
CASE STUDIES

INTRODUCTION

The particular case studies that follow are not scattered indiscriminately through the varied work of an English department exploring reading. There has been an attempt to connect these encounters with fiction to the more coherently organized developmental approach suggested in the companion book, *Continuity in Secondary English*, written by the same author.

Many readers will feel a need at this point for some kind of background information explaining this tentative, developmental approach. (Other readers might like to turn to the much more fully detailed argument and planned framework to be found in the other book.)

(1) Reacting against the often random, *ad hoc* nature of day-to-day teaching (surviving from immediate crisis to crisis) one Midland comprehensive school English department has over the last eight years tried to work out longer-term language development priorities.

(2) It attempted to build, from combined experience, a departmental, developmental framework that started to clear

the ground in front of the teachers so they could concentrate their energies on investigating how children learn and grow through talk, writing and reading from 11 to 18.

(3) They identified four linked but different phases of growth (accepting that these phases often occur in the individual child at different times). These phases represent general tendencies, or possible patterns of development:

(a) *First phase*
Trusting your own voice in an unfamiliar context – 11– 12+ (first year – middle of the second year). At the age of 11, most children have already built up a complex language system which helps them to interpret personal experience. However, many are never given sufficient opportunity to make full use of this language competence. Enjoyment in the more playful uses of language can often help the child to find her full voice in the classroom.

(b) *Second phase*
Expanding perspectives – 12+–14 (upper second year – third year). At this stage children are encouraged to move away from an exclusively egocentric perspective to a position where they are able to view situations from different points of view.

(c) *Third phase*
Reflective awareness – 14–16 (fourth and fifth years). This stage combines the personal fluency of the first phase with the expanded range of the second, and introduces a more careful consideration of language choice which springs from the contract that is made between pupil and teacher.

(d) *Fourth phase*
Thinking aloud in public (sixth form). This phase tries to focus on the learning processes involved in small group talk and informal writing, rather a traditional concern for a didactic teaching style which may not encourage individual interpretation.

(4) We looked for the linking patterns of development between all the four phases that would make the child's growth from 11 to 18 more consistent and coherent, and resources were categorized in terms of the different needs of each phase. (The reading suggestion lists printed at the end of the book also provide an updated version of this, arranged into mainstream/whole class suggestions and class library suggestions that demand a more individual or small group approach.)

The case studies that are included here only work within the first three phases (11–16) of the suggested framework. They are put in here not as a series of tips for teachers but to provoke informed argument, disagreement and future work. Perhaps the most constructive approach is to re-make these suggestions in the light of your own detailed observations of children's work in your own local circumstances.

6
FIRST PHASE:
TRUSTING YOUR OWN VOICE IN
AN UNFAMILIAR CONTEXT
11–12+

Homing in to *The Battle of Bubble and Squeak* (Philippa Pearce) through personal anecdotes

For many 11-year-olds it is not easy to feel at home in the world of school books. They face a wall that divides and breaks up the spoken exuberance, wit, repartee, banter they feel comfortable with in the playground and street of the outside world, from the strange world of print and instructions of the classroom. Viewed directly through pupils' eyes it's like having to cope with two, quite separate lives; outside is a warm, jostling world of immediate encounters and contacts (seething with bad jokes, anecdotes, colloquial bite, crazes, 'Knock, knock/who's there?' games, etc.) often worryingly different from the comparatively remote world of teacher words and book words found in the classroom. It's a transition from speaking to reading (sometimes done in isolation) and also from a world of immediate, concrete approaches to experience to a world that often concerns itself with abstract, detached knowledge.

BUILDING BRIDGES BETWEEN WORLDS: THE BATTLE OF BUBBLE AND SQUEAK

There is a need, then, for teachers to attempt to bring together these two worlds within the classroom; to consciously set out to build reassuring bridges between what the child already knows from his lived experience in the outside world, and the classroom reading experience. Or, as Margaret Donaldson says, to move from 'disembedded' school contexts through to a more 'embedded' approach.[1]

A great deal of teaching in school, she says, is over concerned with 'certain problems which have been "prised out" from the supportive context of the rest of the (pupil's) experience' and she places against this an approach that makes more spontaneous human sense to the child: 'It is when we are dealing with people and things in the context of fairly immediate goals and intentions and familiar patterns of events that we feel most at home.'

It is this translation of the reading experience offered by the school into the 'familiar patterns' and supportive context of the child's everyday language, knowledge and experience that I want to focus on here. And, more particularly, to concentrate on how personal anecdote, a major part of that everyday language, knowledge and experience at this age,[2] can help pupils to make a reading experience their own.

LEARNING AND THINKING THROUGH ANECDOTE

[children] apprehend what others say through story.
(James Moffett, *Teaching the Universe of Discourse*, Boston, Houghton Mifflin, 1968)

Anecdote can be self indulgent. It can be offered up as a

diverting red herring. But it can also act as a means of thinking and learning about classroom experience (in this case encountering fiction).

To the pupils, anecdotalizing is often their most confident and familiar way of homing in to the disturbing newness of a fresh reading experience in the classroom. To take on and possess for themselves the spirit of what they are reading, the pupil has to try and actively fit the unfamiliarity of that experience into her already developed systems of understanding (and especially those organized networks of personal knowledge kept in the mind in the form of anecdotes) so that both the original experience and those existing systems are modified in the process.

So through exchanging anecdotes about a common experience raised by the reading experience they can put their meetings with the book into their own, meaningful currency that they can feel at home with and learn through.

The form was a first year (11- and 12-year-olds) in a 1300 mixed comprehensive school. The children were exploring ways of making sense of the experience of reading *The Battle of Bubble and Squeak* (Philippa Pearce) in an English lesson.

Here are some key moments from the book that catch some of the tension between the mother (who wants to get rid of two newly arrived gerbils and preserve her clean, house-proud order) and her children (who are determined to keep them):
Extracts

(a) The middle of the night, and everyone in the house asleep.

Everyone? Then what was that noise?

Creak! and then, after a pause, Creak! And then, Creak!

And then Creak!

As regular as clockwork —

(b) The creatures had frozen. But Sid himself turned his

head slowly, to see who shone the torch. He said,
'They're gerbils. My gerbils. Mine.'
Bill said: 'Those things?'
'Yes.'
'They were making that noise?'
'Yes. They're not supposed to be up and about at night.
But they are.'
'Like me.'
But Sid rarely smiled at his stepfather's jokes.

(c) '[Mum] was expert at preventing mess.'

(d) 'It's no use your trying to hide them! I saw them!' cried
Mrs Sparrow.
'Rats!'
'No,' said Sid, 'Gerbils.'
'Don't you contradict me at three in the morning', said
Mrs Sparrow.
'They're smelly little rats. Where've they come from?'
'The toolshed.'
'And none of your cheek! Where've they come from?'
'A boy at school gave them to me. Jimmy Dean's
cousin. He gave them to me with the cage, last week. I
put them in the shed. But then the nights began getting
colder. I had to bring them indoors just for the night. I
had to. They're used to hot deserts.'
'They go back to Jimmy Dean's cousin tomorrow
without fail. Today, that is. How many times have I got
to say that we're not having animals in this house?
You've roller-skates and a camera and a transistor:
what more do you want?'

(e) There was a kind of screech from downstairs, and then
the repeated screaming of 'Sid! Sid! Sid!'
It was frightening.
In his school trousers and his pyjama top, Sid flew
downstairs. His mother met him at the bottom of the

stairs. Tears were streaming down her cheeks; she also looked unspeakably angry. 'Come and see what your – your T H I N G S have done!'

She dragged him into the living-room. The room was still in semi-darkness because the curtains had not yet been drawn back. But the gloom was shot by strong beams of light coming through two large ragged holes in the curtains. The holes were just behind the cage, and by the light through them Sid could see that the inside of the gerbil cage was littered with scraps and crumbs of scarlet. One gerbil, sitting up watchfully, seemed to be wiping its mouth free of a scarlet thread. 'They've eaten my best curtains', said Mrs Sparrow.

And finally, a moment that deals with Bill's (the step-father's) search for Sid after he has run away in blind anger from his mother who, unknown to him, has got rid of his two pet gerbils while he was away at school:

(f) The outer parts of the wood seemed haunted by the sharp-edged, painful ghosts of people's worn out metalware. When he moved again, he trod on some-thing that thereupon rose up out of the wintry under-growth like a snake rearing to strike: an old bicycle mudguard. Soon he saw ahead of him, like some sunken hovel, the dumped car that Dawn Mudd had mentioned. All the doors were off. The sickening smell of rot and rust from inside made him certain that Sid was not sheltering there.

He penetrated farther into the wood – farther probably, than most people bothered to go who were dumping rubbish. He could feel round him that the trees were growing closer together. The brambles seemed to spring at least waist high. They seemed deliberately to tear at him. He tripped on a low one, and put his hand out to steady himself on an upright darkness that must be a tree. He felt the tree trunk quite solid under his hand, but then it seemed to move away from him. In terror he stumbled forward. He recovered himself, and realized that this really was only a tree: it had died, or been felled by the wind, but could not fall because of closely surrounding trees. It was supported by its companions, dead on its feet, the corpse of a tree.

He wished that he had brought his torch with him into this wood. Really, he could see nothing; and he could hear nothing except his own crashing about and his own uneven breathing. When he stood still and listened to his breathing, it struck him as sounding like the breathing of a frightened man.

He tried to quiet himself, so that he could listen for noises outside himself, beyond himself. He strained his ears to hear the faintest, most distant sound in the wood, that might be Sid.

But Sid might not be here after all. It was ridiculous of him to have paid any attention to Dawn Mudd. What could she know?

Or, if Sid had come here, he might have gone by now. He might have left the wood as Bill himself had entered it, under cover of all the noise that Bill had been making.

There might be no Sid. He might be quite alone in the wood.

Then, much, much closer that he could ever have expected it, came Sid's voice. It sounded thin and hard. Very unpleasant.

'I've got a knife', said Sid.

I left four pupils alone with a tape recorder and asked them to make sense of their reading of the whole book. They shut themselves away in the room where we keep the English stock and made a forty-minute-long tape. They came out when they thought they had finished.

Later, when I listened to the tape the most noticeable feature was the group's natural tendency to anecdotalize into the text, especially when exploring moments of intense feeling in the story. The teacher's 'making sense' was synonymous to the pupils with matching up their own small story incidents against particular moments in the text:

Pupil 1 '... I like the bit about eating the curtains...'.
Pupil 2 '... that was good...'.
Pupil 3 '... that was early on though...'.
Pupil 4 '...that happened in our caravan when the mice chewed our caravan curtains ... it was terrible...'.

BUILDING CONFIDENCE WITHIN THE CHILD IN THE CLASSROOM

I also asked the same first-year group to jot down their immediate impressions of the book in their reading journals. Here are a few of those rough impressions:

(A) With Mrs Sparrow getting rid of the gerbils without the children knowing makes me think of how my mum got rid of our cat called Sooty. It was a lovely cat but quite vicious because when I wore thick wool socks it used to attack them when I was wearing them so my Mum had to buy me a whole new set of thin socks. But when we going to move it was a few days before our next door but one neighbours cat died. To start with that one was called Sooty but Dale's little sisters Kay and Claire couldn't say Sooty but said Suky so it began to be called Suky instead. So when it died we gave our cat to him. Mum gave it him when we were at school. We were upset but we knew really that Sooty would only try to go back to our old house back at Blidworth and he might get killed on his journey so we gave it to Dale Ashley's family. I wondered whether my Sooty's still alive, I hope so.

(LOUISE MARRIOT)

(B) I remember when I went downstairs on Christmas morning with my brothers to open my presents. Also when I went down the stairs, the stairs creaked. And the bit where they heard the noise. Well I remember when I was in bed and I heard a noise that sounded like footsteps. I got up, looked out the window but there was nothing. And another thing the bit where the mother was shouting at Sid because he had got pets in the house. Well I remember when I wanted a puppy, and my mum said 'if you think you gonna get one of them, you've got another thing coming'. But about a year after that we got one. In the morning at my house, it's just a right mess, Michael's moaning about his breakfasts not ready, Dad's moaning about his tea's cold. And Dad's moaning at me because I haven't cleaned my shoes, and Mum's in a panic.

(SANDRA DAINTY)

In many classrooms the child is made to feel as if she does not exist. Dominated by the teacher's carefully regulated directions she might sometimes feel that she is invisible. And if she feels that her independent existence doesn't matter in the everyday affairs of the classroom she is likely to react passively.

Anecdote can have an important part to play in countering some of these negative tendencies. It can help to establish, within the pupil, a sense that she does exist in relation to the classroom experience introduced by the teacher and that the things that she already knows matter. Because so much of her self-respect and personal confidence in the outside world is bound up with these anecdotes, for the teacher to bring pupil anecdotalizing into the centre of classroom activities is, often to boost pupil morale and increase their motivation.

Louise's Sooty story ('I wondered whether *my* Sooty's still alive ...') is perhaps encouraging her to become actively involved in bringing her own experience to bear on trying to understand what's going on in the book.

The pupils' anecdotes often validate and encourage an immediacy of felt contact between the child's world and the world of the reading experience that no other mode of thinking seems to make possible.

Just look again at the taped comment of these first-formers putting themselves into the position of the children in the book:

Pupil 1 '... I know how they feel because we're going to get a dog but Mum doesn't want us to ...'.

Pupil 2 '... they won't let me have any pet ... you see we had a dog before ...'.

Pupil 3 '... my dad wasn't going to let me have guinea pigs ... you see ... and was ... but I asked him and I asked him and I asked him ... and he let me ...'.

Pupil 1 '... we had a dog last time and he was really wonderful ... but Mum and Dad won't let us have one this time because they say it's too much fuss and everything ...'

The anecdotal mode seems to tap pressures of feeling ('I asked him and I asked him and I asked him ...') in a more direct way than other modes, and also allows the pupils to express those pressures more openly and unguardedly.

CENTRIFUGAL VERSUS CENTRIPETAL ANECDOTES

However, all this sounds a bit too rosy. It has to be admitted that some anecdotes, although important in raising the self-esteem of the child, tend to lead away from the subject, like a centrifugal force flying off from the centre.

The associative power of Rachel's anecdote is valuable and it helps her to enter into the spirit of the book but does it illuminate more clearly the focus of the book, or carry her more deeply into the heart of the reading experience?

Rachel I once had a hamster ... and I wanted to let it run in the bathroom ... thinking there was no holes ...

so I let it go ... and then all of a sudden it
disappeared ... I couldn't see where it was ... it
had disappeared down this hole behind the toilet
... and I never saw it again ... but my Mum knew
where it was ... about a month later she told me
what had happened ... she said that our cat had
got it ... and she found it headless ... underneath
the laurel bush in the garden.

But others act as developing conversations between the
pupil's already existing framework of understanding and the
world of the book:

Jason   two hamsters ... so we asked me Mum and she says,
'Yes', so we went into town that day ... and asked
for some hamsters ... and they gave us two ... one
was all different colours ... and one was brown ... I
had the brown one ... and after a few weeks they
mated and had about seven babies and after about
six weeks we left them out ... at night ... and my
Mum and Dad went into the room while we was in
bed ... and all of a sudden ... they heard this
scratching noise underneath ... and then they heard
it scrambling over the hearth ... so my Mum got the
poker ... and hit it ... and missed it and then she
saw one come out ... then she saw two ... even
three, then four and there was a kind of army of
them coming across the hearth ... then they went
near the curtains and they came out again ... she
went and had a look round the curtains ... and there
was this little hole ... like there was in the *Battle of
Bubble and Squeak* ... and when she caught them all
... she was wearing gloves ... she got no end of bites
on her hands ... and then we sold them after that
because we were getting sick of them running away.

The anecdote here is acting more in a centripetal way; as a
movement into the centre of what he has just read. Jason is

actively making his own meaning out of extracts (a) and (e) above by re-shaping the reading experience of threatening noises (the repetition of 'Creak?') into his own familiar terms ('scratching noise'/'scrambling') that he understands immediately.

There are clear differences between Jason's anecdote and extract (e) from the *Battle of Bubble and Squeak* (Mum and her children seem to be working with each other more) but emotional parallels are being built. Even though the anecdote is deliberately constructed out of what he was told (how could he have experienced it if he was in bed?) and elaborately embroidered, it gives Jason an opportunity to create bridges between the felt dislocation and distress of the mother in extract (e) and his own mother experiencing similar kinds of things in:

'... so my Mum got the poker ... and hit it ... and missed it ...' and '... she got no end of bites on her hands ... and then we sold them after that'.

As well as the explicit attempt to refer back to the story in, 'like there was in the *Battle of Bubble and Squeak* ...' there is probably a closer sense of felt correspondences than in Rachel's anecdote.

The recurring difficulties are mainly about balance; how does the pupil develop a sense of just congruity between the world of the book and her own personal world of understanding? Anecdotes sometimes blur rather than sharpen the focus of understanding, as in Rachel's case.

Let us have a final look at what the pupils made of extract (f) – the description of Bill's eerie search for Sid in the wood:

Pupil 1 ... there's another bit of the book that I thought was really good ... and that's the description of the woods ... with the ... you know ... when he bumped into the tree and it fell over him (laughter).

Pupil 2 ... that scared me and I was only reading it ... that really terrified me ...

Pupil 1 ... you really get the atmosphere there ...

Pupil 3 ... yea because I was reading it in bed and I looked outside and I imagined a great, big wood ... with this man walking through it ...

Pupil 2 ...yea but when I was a bit younger ... I used to sorta ... when I was coming home late ... with only street lights ... I used to see my own shadow ... and then I was always looking back ... to see if there was another ... you know ... you seemed to imagine things ... like he was imagining things in the wood wasn't he?

Pupil 1 ... but that description was fantastic ... very realistic ...

Pupil 2 ... you got into it at that bit didn't you ... you really did get into it ...

Pupil 1 ... I catch its smell ... the leaves ... and all the dampness ... you can imagine the fog sitting there ...

I think the first thing to say about this transcript is that Pupil 2's anecdote ('yea but when I was a bit younger...') does not stay limited within the circle of personal identification but reaches out towards a more complex awareness of the detailed interaction between the 'me'[3] and the 'that', needed to create meaning out of what you read.

His personal insight ('I used to see my own shadow ... and then I was looking back ... to see if there was another...') does illuminate and define more precisely the nature of the correspondence between his own fears and Bill's terrified projection of feelings onto objects in the outside world (e.g. mudguard/brambles, tree trunk). Also, through the establishing of his own personal context for the story episode he is able to think more clearly and explicitly about what's happening to Bill: '...you seemed to imagine things ... like he was imagining things in the wood wasn't he?...'.

The other main point I want to make here is about the coming together in the children's talk of personal reactions and more detached modes of thinking. Evaluative remarks and the more considered comments about the way the book is written (about atmosphere and scene setting) are not severed from the anecdotal response. The children are moving, falteringly, towards a more unified approach where the more formal, stylistic points about the story as artefact are still saturated with direct, personal feelings. And I think the influence of the anecdotalizing has made that possible.

Many teachers and schools then, are underestimating what their pupils already have within them for making sense of their reading encounters in the classroom especially in the first years of the secondary school when children need to feel confirmed in what they already possess. Anecdote, along with other modes of personal knowledge, has a contribution to make to the pupils' learning, enjoyment and understanding of what they read. But at the moment it's often neglected, or dismissed as being marginal.

Perhaps only when teachers start to recognize and respect children's already existing networks of understanding and set out to build bridges between those networks and the world of the school book will more pupils view reading fiction as a nourishing and pleasurable activity.

Learning to become an active reader

Many children can read at 11 but have not learnt the habits of an active reader. Often they feel insecure, not knowing what's expected of them and not really seeing themselves in a future role of confident, fluent readers who can question and make sense of what they read by themselves. Many English departments still feel that these active habits are caught, intuitively, by children meeting a wide range of books, rather than taught explicitly; so that often pupils do not receive any supportive guidelines about how to approach their reading, and advice on how to improve.

What one English department in a 1300 mixed comprehensive school in Nottinghamshire tries to do to combat these negative tendencies is to blend together the reading for pleasure incentive with an actively questioning reading method to encourage readers to go it alone. The selection of reading material is clearly crucial.

CHOICE OF MATERIAL THAT MOTIVATES READERS' INTERESTS

We spend a great deal of time as a department searching for books and stories that speak directly to pupils' often irreverent, humorous world-views; varying from the Viola Angotti episode from *The Eighteenth Emergency* (Betsy Byars), George Layton's short stories *The Shrinking of Treehorn* (F.P. Heide), through to the authentic dialogue of the opening of *Challenge in the Dark* (Robert Leeson) and the raft-building episode of *Private – Keep Out!* (Gwen Grant). Perhaps the most fruitful starting point is working on pupils' incentives for reading so that they can develop the habit of associating print with pleasure. This is particularly important for the children who have personal histories of failure and struggle in learning to read, print often being connected in their minds with an automatic, negative experience.

Building up this positive expectation about reading in English is a gradual process but it is best encouraged through providing a continuously rich and nourishing experience of telling, listening to and reading stories in the classroom. For 11-year-olds personal anecdotes can flow into the world of their reading and vice versa.

Short stories that can be read and completed within one period can be extremely useful with inexperienced readers. A wide variety of memorable stories from folk, fairy and legend collections as well as from specific genres like ghost or science fiction stories or contemporary collections are needed: powerful stories that possess the reader's imagination like 'The Green Children' retold by Robert Scott (from *The Red Storyhouse*), 'The boy who found fear at last' by Andrew Lang (*Olive Fairy Book*), 'The farmer and the snake' by Julius Lester (from *The Kneehigh Man and Other Stories*), 'The Bear-Man' by R. Squires (from *Wizards and Wampum*); stories designed to make the listener jump at a startling ending like 'The old man at the White House', 'Peggy with the wooden leggy' and 'The golden arm' (all from Katherine Briggs' *A Dictionary of British Folktales*), as well as better known collections like 'The Hobyahs' and 'Mr Miacca' (from *English Fairy Tales* by Joseph Jacobs); and stories that respect the independent nature of girls, as in Alison Lurie's re-telling of 'Manka and the judge' (in *Clever Gretchen and Other Forgotten Folktales*).

Original stories with the haunting resonance of 'The shadow cage' (Philippa Pearce) should not be relegated to the end of the afternoon relaxation time after the 'bread and butter' work but given a central prominence in English work with the teacher frequently reading to the whole group.

ABSORBING A QUESTIONING APPROACH INTO THE MAINSTREAM OF READING

Given that a story is chosen with enough power and quality to keep the reader's motivation high do we just read it and leave it at that? Certainly many times we will want to leave the story alone and allow the story to make its claim on the reader's imagination unmediated by the teacher's influence. But, occasionally we will also want to blend together the reading for pleasure incentive with an active, questioning approach where the teacher might play a more developed, guidance role.

Elsewhere[4] I have shown how the department was initially influenced by some of the reading development strategies that were suggested by the *The Effective Use of Reading*[5] and how later we had doubts about isolating a structure of reading development guidance from pupils' more spontaneous intentions and motivations in their everyday reading.

In the current 'back to basics' climate there seemed to us a real danger of these useful methods hardening into mechanical, crossword puzzle procedures that might not affect pupils' general approaches to reading in other, more purposeful situations and their views of themselves as readers. We also wondered whether an isolated reading development programme sometimes neglected the pupils' real purposes for reading (i.e. as indicated above – a rare willingness to be engaged in completely satisfying stories read for pleasure).

This is the background thinking that informed the direction of this case study. I want to go on to investigate an attempt to absorb this active, questioning approach into the mainstream of what we do in the English classroom in order to try to help children to learn the habits of active reading.

PREDICTING INTO 'THE TURBULENT TERM OF TYKE TILER'

Prediction is the basis of human understanding. In order to make sense of confusing experiences we order them into linked webs of meaning. Just as in life, in the world of stories the reader uses what has been read to generate patterns of expectation about possible outcomes and how the story will fit together as a whole. And these anticipatory systems will be modified as new clues are encouraged.

The reading development strategy of group prediction,[6] of encouraging children to decide and to justify what is going to happen next in a selected and edited story can, if the story is worth speculating about, provoke those already existing processing devices in children to help them to actively create their own meanings out of what they read. So it was a particularly suitable approach to apply to a whole book (in this case *The Turbulent Term of Tyke Tiler*) in the effort to encourage a group of first formers to become independent, responsive readers.

There is no doubting the fresh immediacy of the book's appeal to 11-year-olds (the trick riddles, the solidly recognizable worlds of school – 'All the people who come to see him at school to give him tests, the deaf lady, the talk lady, the shrinko chap . . .' – and the comically observed details of what children get up to, as in the account of the contents of Pitthead's pockets – 'three marbles, a packet of chewing gum, an Action Man battle-dress, two bus tickets, and a mini bald koala bear'), but the special narrative strategy used by Gene Kemp in the book gave added point to the prediction approach. The unexpected ending deliberately used the reader's stereotypical expectations to focus on the book's pattern of meaning and values.

The book revolves around Tyke Tiler's last term at junior school and the constant trouble she gets into trying to rescue Danny Price, a likeable but dependent friend, from a variety of tight corners (mostly created by Danny himself). The unexpected climax of the book in the last chapter usually surprises the reader, with its revelation about Tyke's real sexual identity, into reconsidering what has gone before.

I read the book with this particular group over a period of three weeks, sometimes reading two or three chapters to them, at other times asking them to get up to a particular place by reading so many pages for homework. Three times I paused during the reading and asked them to comment on the action and to talk through their predictions about the possible ending of the story, I got them all to promise that they would not take a crafty peek at Chapter Fourteen and the Postscript before we all arrived there naturally. During the pauses I asked them to work in small groups of three or four using the whole classroom space. The physical arrangement of stackable tables and plastic chairs organized into a boardroom square helped them to move into small groups without any great movement of furniture and commotion.

In the first pauses for prediction work the pupils were having the chance to generate expectations about the characters of Tyke and Danny, the nature of their relationship, and how both these factors might affect the outcome of the story. But for our purposes here I want to concentrate on the pupils' final response – their reactions to the surprise ending.

After reading Chapter Fourteen (the surprise ending)

(T = Teacher,   J = Jackie,   S = Samantha,   P = Peter, R = Richard)

T. What's the writer been trying to do?
P. Deceive us.
R. He's tried to keep it all back until the last bit . . .
P. He puts a big question mark at the end . . . for people to really think about it . . .
J. I don't like books like that . . .
T. In thinking about it what have you discovered?
S. Maybe he just thinks Tyke is really a girl because she fancies Danny . . .
T. Does the relationship between Danny and Tyke change now?
P. Well I don't know but his parents must have known that he was a girl . . . why do the parents want him to be a boy?
T. But are there any clues that her parents want her to be a boy? Where does this Tyke name come from rather than Theodora . . . ?
S. I think he's acted a bit too much . . . I don't think he should have acted like a boy . . . because I mean why?
J. Because he wants to . . . I know plenty of girls who are tomboys . . . well if they want to be a boy then they act like a boy don't they? If they don't want to be a girl then they act like a boy . . .
T. Do you think it's only boys who want to climb things?

J. No I wanted to go and thump a teacher before now ...
who really got on my nerves. I wanted to go and scream
at 'im ...

S. I wanted to scream at my mum sometimes but I haven't
had the nerve ...

T. So why have you got to think of Tyke in terms of being
a boy?

J. ... don't know but the author made it out that he was a
boy ... *she* was a boy ...

T. So why did the author write it like that?

J. Dunno ... maybe just to put a question mark at the
end ...

T. What's the question mark about then?

J. Whether he's a boy or she's a girl ...

T. Why did Gene Kemp write it like that?

J. Probably just proving a point by writing a book ...

T. What's the point?

J. Equality isn't it?

S. The author's trying to tell children that they can be the
same or sometimes other way round or not really the
other way round because they're the same ...

P. She's trying to say what is the difference between boys
and girls ... some boy's can be really soft ... some play
football ... you know ... everything ...

R. She nearly gives it away ... she says, 'she used my real
name ... the one I really hate ...'

R. But a girl wouldn't go down for those bones in the river.

J. She would if she was a tomboy ...

T. Why have you got to use the word 'tomboy'?

J. That's just another way of saying the girl's like a boy ...

T. But why can't girls just like doing adventurous things
just like boys?

J. It depends on their personality ...

R. I don't think even a tomboy would go to a deserted mill
on a pitch black night ...

J. ... it depends on how much they wanted to be a boy ...

if they really desperately wanted to prove themselves as
a boy then they'd go and do anything like that . . .

T. So what's the author doing here then?

P. Mixing it all round . . .

J. Swapping it all up to make us all confused . . . to have to
talk about if you have to say 'she', 'he'.

S. Yea and it gets you puzzled – and you don't really know
and it sort of gets you.

J. You have to think about it to understand it . . . usually
you can just read through the endings . . . and then you
just go over the book in your mind . . . but now you have
to figure it out . . . and kind of read the book again to
remind yourself of all the things . . . and to see if you can
get any clues . . .

R. It might make you read all the book again . . . to read it
more properly . . .

S. . . . people have just sort of . . . through the generations
grown up believing boys are like so and so . . . and they
like to climb trees and all the rest of it . . . and girls are
the opposite . . . and play with soppy little dolls . . . and
all the rest of it . . . she's trying to prove that they're not
like in Victorian times . . . she's trying to prove that
they're not . . .

J. The book really strings you along . . . and then at the
very last chapter it *springs* it on you . . .

T. For what purpose?

R. It makes it like a surprise . . . he's a girl . . .

J. Make you think about it . . . it's a main thing . . .

P. It has to be like that at the end because the book . . . it's
interesting . . . but it's only got little titchy bits . . . but it
hasn't got any main thing . . . and it has to have that at
the end . . . something big . . .

T. So why does Gene Kemp write it like that then?

S. She's trying to change your opinion . . . of thinking that
girls are soppy and they don't do anything darey . . . or
anything . . . and she's saying that they do . . . 'cos my

sister ... sometimes I forget she's a girl ... and I think
she's a boy ... because she wants everything boys have.
T. Such as?
S. I asked her what she wanted for her birthday ... and she
said she wanted some Forest sweat bands ... and she
goes around climbing trees and everything...
P. We had this girl at our other school ... right? ... the
boys just got used to her ... she used to play football
with us...
J. Well we used to play football ... me and Lucy Atkin...
P. But this girl ... she used to come out every single time
... she was good at it you know.
J. Yea we used to have scraps with the boys just to show
them that we weren't soppy...

As we build up a consistent network of expectations in
responding to the story we often encounter breaks or
uncertainties in the text that force us to stand back and reconsider and revise the pattern.[7] This is an important growth
point in learning to become independent readers because
these breaks often provoke the active participation of the
reader in having to repair these gaps in understanding.

So here we find the group temporarily floundering at first
because the unexpected ending doesn't fit in to their predicted
outcomes (Samantha: 'I thought Danny was going to go up
there not him.') and a sulky refusal to acknowledge Tyke's
real identity ('Is she thinking of his sister?'). But gradually the
truth dawns on them and in trying to re-adjust to this sudden
shift of viewpoint and expectations the pupils are pushed
back to look more closely at the text. So Richard, retrospec-
tively, goes back to the text with a much more detailed
scrutiny: ('She nearly gives it away ... she says, "she used my
real name ... the one I really hate...".'). They also reconsider
key moments in the story, like the bones episode and the
deserted mill bit, within a fresh perspective, and begin to
recognize that 'swapping it all up to make us all confused'

leads them on to 'figuring it out' for themselves. As Jackie says, you're motivated to 'read the book again to remind yourself of all the things ... and to see if you can get any clues...'. And a fuller, more questioning reading approach can develop out of this second look; as Richard suggests, 'It might make you read all the book again ... to read it more properly...'.

Closely tied in to these narrative dislocations and a reader's connected revisions is a moral questioning. The unexpected ending challenges and confronts the reader's habitual values and use of familiar sexist stereotypes.

Arthur Applebee in his *Child's Concept of Story*[8] has shown us how very young children have already picked up stable expectations about roles, behaviour and stock characters. And viewed from one angle this can be a constructive part of the reader's processing of the unfamiliar into coherence. But from another viewpoint these stable, predictable expectations can prove diminishing and suffocating.

Part of the equipment of an active reader is the ability to interrogate these received stereotypes as part of reading for meaning. The teacher's role in this is to make a more informed choice of stories or fictions that challenge received habits of thought in the way they are put together so that the reader will be more regularly invited to participate in the making of meaning with the author.[9]

The shocking unexpectedness of the role reversal in the ending ('the book really strings you along — and then at the very last chapter it *springs* it on you...') stirs the pupils up into a detailed re-examination of their familiar stereotypes.

At first they negatively measure Tyke up against their narrowly restrictive anticipations about boys defining themselves as boys through their apparently sole possession of an independently robust energy: 'He's acted like a boy ... in real life you can tell what they're like by the way they act...', but through having a chance to match up their own diverse personal experience ('No I wanted to go and thump a teacher before now ... boys can be really soft ... some play football...') against these received notions pupils like Jackie and Samantha start to see more clearly what's going on in the book.

Earlier, because she was flummoxed, Jackie had dismissed the story out of hand with, 'I don't like books like that...', but through the confirming strength of the evidence of her own personal stories she begins to twig what the point of the story is about: 'Equality isn't it?'

Samantha is even more lucid; she also started in some confusion ('I don't think he should have acted like a boy ... because I mean why?'...) but she talks herself towards a position of real understanding: '...people have just sort of ... through the generations grown up believing boys are like so and so ... and they like to climb trees and all the rest of it ... and girls are the opposite ... and play with soppy little dolls ... she's trying to prove that they're not like in Victorian times...'.

At the end of the discussion Samantha seems to have fully appreciated the writer's intentions, realising that the story is shaped like that to confront the reader's ingrained sexist assumptions: 'She's trying to change your opinion ... of thinking that girls are soppy and they don't do anything darey ... and she's saying that they do ... cos my sister ... sometimes I forget she's a girl – and I think she's a boy ... because she wants everything boys have.'

Samantha's revaluations are struggling to emerge, breaking through a dead crust of second-hand opinion and negative cultural stereotype ('...sometimes I forget she's a girl ... and I think she's a boy...') but at least they're taking shape. She's on the way to behaving like an active reader, both engaging with the story personally and 'figuring it out' for herself. And, hopefully, on the way she's learning a transferable habit that she can apply to other classrooms, contexts and reading experiences. And that might even affect the way she sees herself and her place in the outside world.

Notes

1   Margaret Donaldson, *Children's Minds*, London, Fontana, 1978.
2   See 'Dignifying anecdote', *English in Education*, Spring 1983, for supporting arguments and a much more fully developed treatment of the educational value of anecdotes.
3   See D.W. Harding's comment on this: '. . . our aim is to move dynamically from the "me" of personal identification to the "that" of the poem or object in the poem. The discipline lies in the attentiveness to the "that" and it should be made plain that there is no dichotomy here, but a natural movement from subject to object and back again' (from 'Response to literature', in Margaret Meek, Aidan Warlow and Griselda Barton (eds), *The Cool Web*, London, Bodley Head, 1977).
4   *Continuity in Secondary English*, London, Methuen, 1982.
5   Eric A. Lunzer and Keith Gardner (eds), *The Effective Use of Reading*, London, Heinemann, 1979.
6   See the paper 'Improving reading through group discussion activity', in *The Effective Use of Reading*.
7   See Wolfgang Iser, 'The reading process: a phenomenological approach', in Jane P. Tomkins (ed.), *Reader-Response Criticism*, Baltimore, Md, Johns Hopkins, 1980.
8   University of Chicago Press, 1978.
9   See some of Ernest Hemingway's short stories, e.g. the opening and ending of 'The end of something' and 'Cat in the rain'; *Slake's Limbo* by Felice Holman; 'Computers don't argue' by Gordon Dickson (in *Story Three*); *Z for Zachariah* by Robert C. O'Brien; 'First men on Mercury' by Edwin Morgan (in *Worlds*, ed. G. Summerfield).

7
SECOND PHASE:
EXPANDING PERSPECTIVES
12+–14

Mastering new forms through reading and writing

Many 13- to 14-year-olds seem to stagnate in the secondary English classroom. Often made uncertain and awkward because of their own physical changes and their transitional role in the school (juniors no longer but not yet seniors) many pupils feel they are just marking time. Paul, who is often listless and spends most of his ingenuity trying to avoid work, put it well when he commented on English in the third year, 'It's just doing the same old things over and over again.'

This wish to do something different and more demanding in this phase needs to be listened to more seriously and responded to by English teachers. There is a need to find ways of helping the pupil to extend her range and techniques as a reader and writer of fiction.

If the pupil is not to go on merely treading water week after week then it is really important to investigate how pupils can be motivated to want to master new forms and competences through their reading and writing and, more particularly, how they can gain more conscious control over the mechanics of story-making (i.e. how stories can be organized to fit together in different ways) so that their reading and writing of stories can become more effective.

This progressive mastery of the tacit rules, systems and conventions of fiction should be more at the heart of what we do in the English classroom between the second half of the second year and the end of the third year. As a way of explaining and developing this statement I want to take a look at a group of third-formers considering the new crafting options available to them through investigating different ways of telling a story.

It was late in the third year and I wanted to move into approaching *I Am the Cheese* (Robert Cormier). Although used to a more kaleidoscopic approach to narrative form from their television watching, many third-formers are often surprised to meet that kind of approach on the page. Rarely having had the chance to pause, share or reflect (or in televisual terms – to freeze the film, replay and ponder together) on such a bewildering device of running three stories together at the same time, I planned a more gradual way in through a short story called 'The boy, the dog and the spaceship' (Nicholas Fisk), a story that involved some of the same narrative techniques used in *I Am the Cheese*.

I explained that we were going to spend the next month considering how stories could be put together in different ways through their own reading and writing activities, and that I wanted them to record in their reading journals what their impressions of the story were as we went through it. I also paused several times through the story and tape-recorded their immediate responses.

I want to focus my attention on the work of one small group of two boys and two girls – Peter, Simon, Mandy and Lindsay. Here are a few pieces from Mandy's and Lindsay's journal reactions.

(A)

The story is like two separate stories, one of a space ship and another of a boy and his dog. It makes you wonder when they're going to meet and how they're going to meet because we had been reading from the boy's point of view, as a human sees it, it doesn't occur to you that the thing in the space ship isn't human or the same size as we are. Although we should have thought something was fishy when the boy didn't see the spaceship. You don't really realize until he sees a dense forest of green columns and green roots with yellow platforms at their summits and then it strikes you that he must only be a few millimetres tall.

When you know he's so small you don't think he would be capable of taking over the world. Then when the captain manages to get in the dog's ear, you begin to have doubts especially when he makes the dog attack the boy. It isn't until the boy hits the dog's ear and the captain falls out, wounded, that you can sigh a sigh of relief.

I think that the way this story is put together makes you think a lot more. It makes the story a lot more interesting to read. You don't just read through it, bored, you have to stop and think. I think the story helps too. This story wouldn't have been so good if it was from one point of view and I think some stories wouldn't be so good written like this.

I can't recall coming across a story like this before. I think we ought to be introduced to different ways of writing stories because it would help us write better stories.

(MANDY TOOLEY)

(B)

Nearer the middle of the story, I kept trying to anticipate what was going to happen. To me, it was quite obvious that eventually, both their paths would cross. And with this in mind, I tried to think ahead and decide how they would meet.

It came as quite a surprise to find out that the spaceship plus captain were tiny, but if I had read more carefully, I would have noticed the fact that only the dog noticed the spaceship. (If it had been of any size, Kevin would have noticed too!) I enjoyed the part where he knew that they were about to meet but you didn't know where or how.

The way the story was put together made me think more. I enjoyed it this way. It wasn't that different, strange at first, but when you understood it, you followed easily.

(LINDSAY GASKELL)

And here are two extracts from the transcript of the discussion with a teacher.

'The boy, the dog, the spaceship'

(1)

T. What differences are there?

M. Well, it's taking two different stories at once and talking about one story and then going over to the other one...

T. How does that make the reader differ in her reactions to the story?

P. Well you're thinking when it's going to come together ... you're thinking when the ship lands he's going to see the ship – or whatever...

T. So what's the connection between these two stories? That's the major problem asked by this.

P. You think they're going to meet.

T. Why do you think they are?

L. They've got to be connected in some way.

T. What are the hints and clues then?

P. The way he's playing with his dog outside the field ... in an open space away from most people ... and the way the spaceship's going to crash and they don't really know where ... so it's going to be very random...

L. ... probably going to be in that field.

T. It's a different form of story telling isn't it?

    L. We've never been told how to write a story, like you
    write it like this ... we've just been told, 'Go ahead and
    write a story about such and such...'.

(2)
    T. What's exactly happening here?
    M. The thing he's talking about doesn't seem to be Earth
    ... well to us it sounds as if he's climbing up grass ...
    and plants ... so he's probably small ... and it doesn't
    give any clues as to what kind of planet he came from
    ... or what size he is...
    T. How is it seen – the story?
    S. Well it's somebody's different angle.
    T. Does that help or hinder the reader?
    P. Well it makes you think about other people's angles ...
    and other things' angles.
    M. First of all ... it didn't occur to you that he was going
    to be a different size or anything ... for you were seeing
    it from the boy's point of view ... and it wasn't green
    and there were just trees and everything ... and when
    he got out it was different completely ... so it made you
    think what was different about him that made him see
    it differently.
    T. Does the different point of view make you think more
    about what you're reading? In the 3rd year do you
    think you ought to read stories like this?
    M. It's better if we get more experience in widening our
    outlook.
    T. I don't really understand what's going on here?
    L. Sounds like dandelions or buttercups with the yellow
    things on top of the grass.
    T. So what size is he then?
    P. He's obviously bigger than most insects ... for it's
    swaying under his weight.

Although some of the remarks, especially Mandy's, are
searching for approval from the teacher, perhaps the most

promising point about these impressions is that there is a growing conscious recognition that the story has been deliberately constructed like that to express the writer's purposes. It did not just turn out like that, spontaneously, but has been thoughtfully composed.

Pupils often agree with Brecht that, 'with works of art[ ] it is impossible to find out how they are made. Those who make them work hard to give the impression that everything just happens, as it were of its own accord ...' and that '... the process of manufacture' rather than the finished product should be focused on more openly.[1] Perhaps teachers of fiction ought to concentrate much more at this stage on making explicit to their pupils the shaping and patterning decisions involved in story-making. As Lindsay says, '... we've never been told how to write a story, like you write it like this ... we've just been told, 'Go ahead and write a story about such and such ...'.

One important aspect of this laying bare of the skeletal form is an understanding of point of view. Simon, Peter and Mandy are able to see that a main part of the writer's intentions in this science fiction story is to subvert the familiar perspective of the boy's (and perhaps reader's) view of what is going on. They are well on the way to standing back from the immediate encounter with the story to reflect more precisely on why this story has been written in the way it has:

T. How is it seen − the story?

S. Well it's somebody's different angle.

T. Does that help or hinder the reader?

P. Well it makes you think about other people's angles ... and other things' angles.

M. First of all ... it didn't occur to you that he was going to be a different size or anything ... for you were seeing it from the boy's point of view ... and it wasn't green and there were just trees and everything ... and when he (the Captain) got out it was different completely ... so it made you think what was different about him that made him see it differently.

An awareness of this alternative perspective ('other people's angles ... and other things' angles') and the non-linear story form ('taking two different stories at once and talking about one story and then going over to the other one...') helps them to appreciate the author's intentions in choosing to collide an invading alien's perceptions against Kevin's and Reg's familiar expectations. Becoming a more mature reader (and then perhaps later, writer) means learning to adapt to different narrative strategies and to see them as a part of the writer's search for a suitable form that will do justice to the meaning of the content and experience. So that Lindsay is able to comment on the story form: 'It wasn't that different, strange at first, but when you understood it, you followed easily.'

MAKING MEANING THROUGH A SENSE OF STORY

As I made clear in the first phase case study on *The Turbulent Term of Tyke Tiler*, a concern with new forms (e.g. stories that have deliberate interruptions to their flow) can also go hand in hand with encouraging pupils to become more effective readers.

In this story the different narratives existing alongside each other, and the shifting point of view, excite the pupils' curiosities about the reasons for such a puzzle, and prompt them to make maximal use of those inner interpretative systems (of which a sense of story is one of the most important in this context) in searching for coherent connections between the apparently separate, random parts of the story: 'It makes you wonder when they're going to meet and how they're going to meet...'.

Reading effectively here means casting backwards and forwards in the story at the same time so that the active efforts of the reader can piece together the single units of the story into a reconstructed unity. Here in their journal and tape comments the pupils are learning to piece together by themselves: 'Nearer the middle of the story, I kept trying to anticipate what was going to happen. To me, it was quite obvious that eventually, both their paths would cross. And with this in mind, I tried to think ahead and decide how they would meet.'

Often involved in this process is a more careful pondering and teasing out of significance for the reader. This more reflective position is shown by Lindsay when she says, '... but if I had read more carefully, I would have noticed the fact that only the dog noticed the spaceship ...'.

The planned uncertainties of these new narrative forms then can, if well crafted, motivate the reader into more complex reflection. As Mandy commented (in a piece not included here in the extracts from the tape transcript): 'Instead of just racing along ... you've got to stop and think what's going to happen next and work it out ...'.

"I AM THE CHEESE" (ROBERT CORMIER)

There were three parts to their approach to this book. Building on their growing awareness of how stories can fit together in unusual ways through their exploration of 'A boy, a dog and a spaceship' they talked through their reactions to the book as they went through it, and finally tried out their own non-linear stories and commented on the process of writing them. I will take these parts, one by one:

(A) *Small group talk as they moved through the book*

(S = Simon, P = Peter, M = Mandy, L = Lindsay)

(1) *Up to page 15*

S. At first I found it a bit confusing.

T. Is it too frustrating to read?

L. I thought it was going to be at first ... an ordinary sort of story ... you know where he's going to meet his father ... there's a bit where he threw the tablets down

the sink ... down the waste disposal ... and you think
that's a bit weird.

M. You wonder why he's got these tablets ... and whether
there's anything wrong with him especially when it
comes to this tape bit ... and whether he's got to see a
doctor ... a psychiatrist or something ... because he's a
bit wappy or something.

L. And why's he going to visit his father?

M. Because they're in it together ... and you don't know
whether the tape's now or before then?

P. That's what I was wondering ... when it went to the
end of the tape ... when he didn't care what ever ...
you wonder whether he's being spied on or something.

L. Sounds as if this is in another century ... you know
what I mean? It sounds a bit like *1984*.

P. And is it a translated story ... all these foreign names.

T. It's just written in America.

T. What was it like as a reader to meet the tapes for the
first time on page 10?

P. You got lost don't you? Trying to follow as from there,
'down into Aswell' (pointing to the page that immediately precedes the first tape) ... but I didn't ... I read
the first bit twice really.

M. You don't know whether it's him thinking it or whether
it's just a new bit ... because it starts on a new page ...
um ... but it's totally different from the story.

L. You suddenly get plunged into a totally different kind
of story ... from being an ordinary ... sort of story ...
you've got this almost play-like thing ... it's almost
thought ... it's a bit of a tape and it's his thoughts as
well ... it's different....

       *   *   *   *

T. Do the tapes make the cycling story different?

M. On this tape ... if it is this boy who's cycling along ...
then it makes you remember the things that sounded a
bit funny about him ... when it describes him ... kind

of thing ... it makes you wonder if something's wrong
with him ... whereas before you just took it as it came
along ... and didn't think there was anything particularly wrong with him.

L. It's strange ... so that you think about things that
weren't quite right with the boy.

P. The only thing that stuck in my mind was the perfume
... the lilac perfume.

T. Lilac perfume and a smell of tobacco from his Dad.

T. What's going on in this boy's mind?

L. It seems as if he's trying to remember what his parents
were like...

M. (confused) As if he's apart from them ... in a house or
something ... it said they were going to send him
away...

L. He's trying to conjure up memories (confused) ... his
last memories...

S. It's his father...

L. What do you mean?

S. He's going to see his father ... I got the impression that
the kid who was doing this was frightened of how it
was ... them smells he was familiar with ... he lost ...
from his family ... and it made him more frightened ...
more confused.

The dislocation between the pupils' linear story expectations and the abrupt interruptions of the tape episodes
provokes their wondering speculations about what's going
on: 'you get lost don't you ... I read the first bit twice
really...' and 'you wonder why he's got these tablets ... and
whether there's anything wrong with him...'. However if
there is too much uncertainty some children will turn away
from the story, too frustrated to want to go on. Here they
start like that and then having the chance to exchange their
queries in a small group allows them to get further involved in
the networking of these random clues into some kind of
coherent order.

This synthesizing centres on the time relations within the story ('you don't know whether the tape's now or before then?') and the possible links between the bike and tape stories.

The pupils, as always, do not just stay with trying to make sense of single, isolated episodes but start to construe what is going on in terms of their familiarity with common literary patterns and themes. Lindsay picks up Peter's reference to 'being spied on' and expands it into, 'it sounds a bit like *1984*' and in section 2 where she goes on to say, 'the story seemed a bit science-fiction'. As Frank Kermode says, she is beginning to 'sense the genre of the utterance' and to interpret the impersonal, medical atmosphere of the tapes through the conventions and rules of the typical science fiction story. Later she will have to modify and revise this interpretation in the light of how the story unfolds but here it is helping her to make sense of bewilderingly fragmentary clues.

The pupils are also further developing their explicit awareness of the story-making process. They are learning to distinguish between the different kinds of discourses used by the bike and tape stories ('... you suddenly get plunged into a totally different kind of story ... from being an ordinary ... sort of story ... you've got this almost *play-like thing* ... it's almost thought...') and are seeing the possible advantages of 'taking two different stories at once' as a fresh narrative method. It is dawning on them that the relationship between the two stories produces an added dimension to the story and to the reader's response: '... then it makes you remember the things that sounded a bit funny about him ... when it describes him ... kind of thing ... it makes you wonder if something's wrong with him ... whereas before you just took it as it came along...'.

(2) *Up to page 27*

T. What did you make of it then?

L. Weird ... the bit where he's in the garage ... and the bit about people listening in to the telephone ... people forging identification ... why should they mention that? (long pause)

L. Well to me the story seemed a bit Science-fiction...

M. Well he's old-fashioned, on a pedal bike and wearing a cap and that's different from the tape bit ... the medication ... that seems futuristic ... and the identification ... I know you're asked for identification in France...

L. Yes, the everyday person who's walking along ... you don't say, 'Can I have your identification please' ... only if it's a policeman who comes to the door...

S. I think his fear of animals is a clue as well...

M. It sounds as if he's nervous of everything ... there doesn't seem to be anything he's not afraid of...

T. How does he cope with that?

M. By not going to those places and trying to avoid everything...

S. It says that he feels secure on his bike...

L. Is it because the bike reminds him of his father?

S. His father's in hospital as well?

P. Why is his father in hospital ... has he got a long-term illness? That's why he had to move?

L. And the bit where it said, '... before my mother became sad...'

M. Sounds as if she's depressed because ... perhaps his father's dying or something ... and because he's been brought up from three and a half ... and his Dad ill ... maybe he's not very secure?

L. He sounds very insecure ... like the bit about the animals...

S. On the tape he seems sad to me ... because in the book ... here it was going on about how he longed to see Amy ... (was it?) this girl ... and on the tape he doesn't want to talk about it anymore.

M. On the tape he's got his mother and father behind him

hasn't he? I think it said that somewhere ... 'I look behind and see them?'

P. You're thinking that this tape ... well I am ... is done ... and in the hospital when he actually arrives there ... and he's going to get dragged into it ...

M. It says, 'Have you administered your medicine today?' ... and that makes you think he hasn't done it today ... maybe it's in the future ...

(3) *Pages 27–85*

P. I think you couldn't write the story in any other way.

T. Why not?

P. The first part I find slightly confusing ... and if it was without a tape ... with no explanation ... without a tape ... it would be very confusing ...

T. Why couldn't you just have had the cycling story?

M. Because then it would miss out the tape then wouldn't it? [laughter]

M. It would ... the majority of things happen in the tape.

L. It's a different way of putting things in the tape.

T. What does the tape give you that the cycle story doesn't?

S. His past ...

L. His thoughts ...

P. The problem is ... how do we know it's his past?

M. In the tape it said ... about when he was four and it said, 'you were four then' ... and then fourteen ... so it's bound to be his past.

P. I'm trying to puzzle out whether it's after the bike ride to Vermont.

S. I think it's before.

P. I think it's after ... because he talks of Amy ... whereas if it was before? Even though I thought it might be before because he was ill ... then I thought he might get worse you see it was very confusing.

L. It might be a long time after because you know at the

beginning it said he didn't want to phone Amy ... and say goodbye or anything?

T. Do you think the past, present and future connections in the story are puzzling or do you think they're deliberately done?

P. I think they're deliberately done...

M. Yea to make you think more.

P. I don't know whether they're there to make you think more?

L. It makes it more interesting to read.

            *   *   *   *

S. I thought if you didn't have the tape it would just be a really boring book ... you know ... the cycle ride ... there wouldn't be much to it at all.

T. How do the two stories link up if at all?

P. I think something's going to happen ... now he's nearing the end of his cycle ride ... and something drastic mentally ... he's going to bang his head or his father's going to say something strange or something odd's going to happen ... and he's going to be admitted to a hospital.

S. I get the impression that he's had a mental breakdown and that ... but my ideas were changing all the way through the book ... first of all I started out thinking that they'd just moved to the hospital ... and then I got the impression that they're on the run ... and his father might be some kind of convict ... then I thought an accident would occur to the boy on his way to see his father and therefore that's why he's doing this hospital thing.

P. ... it makes you wonder about his two birthdays ... the birth certificates and the place calls and all these things.

M. ... you think something really funny's going on ... but you're trying to think what ... but they're not giving you enough clues to grasp what's going on ... you

know you want to carry on reading to find out quick
but it doesn't come like that.

S. What confused me is the doctor ... he's always talking
about clues...

M. Yea ... it's as if he's trying to get something out of the
boy...

S. Yea about his father ... I thought ... somebody had
done his father in ... and that he was trying to find
them...

M. I thought somebody had injured his father ... because
he'd got some information or something ... and they
kidnapped the boy ... and they were trying to get clues
from him ... or something ... then I changed my mind
about that ... because they were giving him medicine
and everything weren't they?

P. Yea ... it seems too good for that ... it could be that
he's just going crazy ... you have to remember that he
was also ill before he was admitted to this hospital ...
on this bike ride ... because he was now wishing he
had taken his pills.

In constantly trying to build bridges between the bike and
tape stories, and organize them into a whole pattern of
meaning, the pupils are being kept on the hook. As Mandy
comments: '... you know you want to carry on reading to
find out quick but it doesn't come like that'. The complicated
time relations and their sense of an emerging contrast between
Adam's wish for security and an alienating strangeness
intrigue them to the extent that they want to find out more.

They are also able to comment on the peculiar appropri-
ateness of the form for the particular needs of the experience
being expressed. ('I think you couldn't write the story in any
other way.') The need to hang on to comforting reassurances
(e.g. Pokey the pig, the plain bike, father's old cap, memories
of Amy Hertz, the lilac perfume and the smell of his father's
tobacco) while Adam is trying to come to terms with a

traumatizing, shattering past gives the split narrative added point.

Some of the pupils also sense the necessary complementarity of the two narratives. Simon and Lindsay realize that the tape episodes bring in reference to Adam's past and his actual thought process so that his fantasy retreat through the bike ride has to come up against the tape revelations about his past that he is trying to repress. They have not articulated it precisely but, stumblingly, they are moving in that direction.

What is important about this is that the pupils are being shown a working example of a writer matching up an original narrative form with the needs of a complex experience. So that, hopefully, their own repertoire of possible techniques and forms is being widened through this reading encounter.

The pupils' sense of the internal rhythm of the story ('I think something's going to happen ... now he's nearing the end of his cycle ride ... and something drastic mentally...') is also becoming sharper. Peter detects signals that the story is about to mount to an explosive climax that will bring together the two narratives: '... he's going to bang his head or his father's going to say something strange or something odd's going to happen ... and he's going to be admitted to a hospital'.

(4) *Up to page 107*

M. Well it's not telling it from the boy's point of view ... somebody else is telling the story ... it's as if the boy's another person ... it's 'he'...

L. I don't know how they put it on to the tape.

P. It seems like ... it's only the author there ... nobody else would know about the number with Amy Hertz.

T. Why does the writer change from the tape way of saying it to the author writing it in this 'Amy and Adam did this...' kind of way?

P. Because Adam doesn't see everything ... Adam doesn't see what his father and mother are doing ... you know

... what's going on ... if it was more in Adam's eyes
you wouldn't get enough information ... you wouldn't
understand what was going on ... like Adam.

*   *   *   *

T. How important is the change from the first person ('I'
telling) on the tape to the third person ('he' telling)?

P. You wouldn't get things like, 'His father must have
sensed his presence' ... through Adam's eyes.

L. You would ... you'd get 'I thought my father knew I
was there ...'

T. Which is better?

M. He (Adam) wouldn't have thought that would he?

(5) *Pages 107–72*

T. Do you think this way of telling is necessary for the
story ... to keep certain things hidden from you the
reader?

P. When you're looking for more information it makes
you want to read on.

T. But can't it irritate you as well?

S. Well when you're reading the tape and you're
getting into it and it comes to the bicycle part ...
that sometimes irritates me.

T. Which pieces do you look forward to reading most?

M./L. The tape.

M. When he's on the bike you can't put any more clues
together to understand what's happening ... it is
just like another story ... you've just got to read that
to find out what's happening.

P. It's little to do with the story I think.

S. I disagree ... I think I enjoy the bicycle part of the
book ...

T. What does the bike bit do that the tape doesn't?

P. I think it pieces the tape together ... if it was just a
plain tape you'd wonder what was going on ... why
was he in hospital ... it gives you an idea ... it

couldn't just be the book with either one of the two
... really it has to be both of them together.

S.   It wouldn't be a very good story if it was just the
      bicycle or the tape.

P.   They both have about things like Amy Hertz and his
      mother.

*   *   *   *

P.   Well it seems a very simple outcome gets contradic-
      ted ... you try and map out what you think's going
      to happen and somehow it's contradicted ... well
      ... you think which comes first ... the cycle story or
      the tape ... then you think do they join on? After
      he's told us about his father ... having an accident
      ... getting shot or blown up or something ... does
      the cycle story come in after that or the tape?

L.   It seems if they're not going to meet ... the only
      connection between the stories is the lad.

P.   There's a time warp at the motel isn't there? He
      thought it was only last summer but it's been closed
      for years ... so was he in hospital *before* the
      journey? And then he thinks he goes in hospital *after*
      the journey.

T.   What are you still puzzling out between pages 107–
      72?

P.   Where are the main connections ... I think it's all
      weird ... you can't see when it will join ... *if* it will
      join ... I think with all the tape now ... it's all a part
      of the scandal to do with his father ... as if it's been
      picked up after the accident.

L.   It sounds as if his father's going to be killed or
      something by the way they went off ... and his
      mother's afraid of that Mr Grey ... and Adam's
      feeling the same kind of thing with the psychiatrist
      ... the same kind of fear ... as if he's out for
      something else ... (Adam) feels that he (the psy-
      chiatrist) isn't there just to help him discover his

past ... he's there to help find out something about his past ... they're not concerned with him but his parents...

T.   What's the difference between the way the tape is written and the way the main cycle story sounds?

L.   The cycle story makes it sound as if Adam is slightly off-centre ... it sounds as if everybody's out to get him ... the tapes ... they use short words ... words you've got to think about ... the meaning doesn't hit you straight away...

T.   What's the impact of the tape on you as a reader?

S.   Talking about the way the tape is written ... the doctor is very efficient ... and he never opposes Adam ... he's always on his side ... that made him seem like a doctor to me.

T.   Did he talk in a doctor way?

L.   At the beginning he did ... like saying, 'Relax...' or 'have a pill' but now he's sort of always getting at him.

P.   To me it's as if he's a part of a mass scandal ... that's really what the story's getting at ... the massive corruption in the US Government ... that's what it strikes me as...

L.   That no matter what you do ... they're still going to get you...

T.   Who's this doctor?

L.   He's a government agent ... trying to find out if Adam knows anymore than his father knew...

By this stage of the book I'd drawn attention to the three different styles being used by Cormier – the first person voice in the bike ride pieces, the tape exchanges, and the third person descriptions of Adam's past that often come immediately after the tape pieces. Encouraged by this, in section 4 we catch the pupils distancing themselves from the immediate push of the story in order to explore style and angle. They are learning about the choices available to the writer, and that these decisions about point of view ('somebody else is telling the story ... it's as if the boy's another person...') and about shifts from first person narration to third person, carry with them certain possibilities that directly affect the kind of story it is.

For example, Peter realizes that a change from the tape to a third person narration allows the reader to see more of what is going on rather than being limited to what can be shown through the perspective of one or two people. He remarks that, '... Adam doesn't see everything ... Adam doesn't see what his father and mother are doing ... if it was more in Adam's eyes you wouldn't get enough information...'. So gradually the pupils are becoming aware of what is really involved in the writer's composing process and the kinds of choices that confront him on every page.

In section 5 the pupils are finally recognizing that the meaning of the whole work comes from the interrelationship between the bike and tape stories ('it couldn't just be the book with either one of the two ... really it has to be both of them together...'). As they near the end of the story they are more confident about pulling the separate clues together into an organized interpretation. They are still puzzling over the 'main connections' and are often forced into an active revision of general theories because of the contradictions but now they are able to discern regularities like Lindsay's discovery that, '... his mother's afraid of that Mr Grey ... and Adam's feeling the same kind of thing with the psychiatrist ... the same kind of fear ... as if he's out for something else...'. And now they can offer informed guesses about the writer's intentions, '... to me it's as if he's a part of a mass scandal ... that's really what the story's getting at ... the massive corruption in the US Government...' and '... no matter what you do ... they're still going to get you...'.

(6) *The ending, pages 172–91* (the end).
(Mandy was not present for this last discussion.)
T. Did you find it a surprising ending?

P. It's built up as though something odd is going to happen ... you're expecting that.

T. Do the two stories come together here?

L. Yes ... well after the accident it's obvious that he wouldn't accept the reality ... and he was put into a hospital ... and he's been there for quite a while.

T. And what's happening in the end to Adam?

L. He's just going to stay there for the rest of his life.

P. He's living his past through again and again ... continually ...

S. I would have thought he would have been ... a yearly cycle.

L. That's the last thing he remembers.

P. And he keeps living that thing through.

T. Can you explain what's happening in the ending?

L. Well it turns out that both his father and mother are dead ... that Mr Grey/Mr Thompson is 2222 (see last tape, pages 188–90) ... because his mother has said that ages ago ... was told by the Mafia ... or whatever it was ... to get rid of him ... well let them know where he was anyway ... if they picked him up ... the lad ... I don't know why they didn't kill him ... but they said he'd be useful.

*   *   *   *

T. Do you think you've learnt anything about how stories are put together?

S. I've certainly learnt a new way of writing them ... I enjoyed this book ... all through this book you were working at it ... trying to think of the ending ... whereas normal you sort of read on.

L. You start out with an aim in mind to find out what was going to happen? ... and with this at the beginning you were given certain things that made you puzzle over them and you wanted to find out what was going to happen.

M. (Having just come back from the dentist) I think that more or less ... because normally I don't think I would have come across stories written in this way ... I usually just read straight stories.

T. Think back to when you were first years ... do you think this is the right way to develop in English ... to read and write stories in a more complex way? Do you think that's what we ought to be teaching in this English department here?

P. Yes but what we do in the Second year and the Third year is very boring ... it's very samey I mean.

T. What's the difference between a first year's way of doing it and a third year way of doing it?

P. Why do we do the same stories ... the story we're reading at the moment is so simple.

L. *Collision Course* it's so predictable ... real rubbish.

P. Not as good as *Bubble and Squeak*.

L. *I Am the Cheese* is much more demanding ... you have to think about what you're reading ... whereas in that *Collision Course* ... you just read it ... and the story just goes on from there ... but this story doesn't just unfold.

M. You have to unfold it yourself...

The pupils are now in a position to build complete structures of meaning from what they've read, as in Peter's remark, '... he's living his past through again and again ... continually...'. That use of 'continually' helps the group to understand the repetitive symmetry of the bike ride but it does not cope with the planned ambivalence of the ending.

Lindsay effectively unravels most of the uncertainties in her contribution starting, '... well it turns out...' but none of the group really does justice to the development within Adam by the end of the story. Perhaps the teacher could have profitably directed attention towards the purging of his past and more mature acceptance of his own solitary position reflected in the completion of the childhood song, 'The cheese stands alone', and later, '... I know, of course, who I am, who I will always be. I am the cheese.'

There seems to me to be a new sense of stability and self-understanding in that 'always' that might lead a reader to viewing the repeated bike ride of the ending not as a negatively obsessive fantasy ritual but perhaps as an actual, independent journey this time. Of course there's a deliberate ambiguity in this ending. The reader is not supposed to close it down too neatly but to go on speculating after the book is finished. And that is perhaps what the teacher should have encouraged more purposefully.

What have the pupils gained from this? As they recognize this second phase can be 'very samey', merely a wishy-washy continuation of what they are already familiar with from the first phase without creating more complex demands upon them as readers and writers. So a great deal depends upon the teacher's selection of materials.

As well as books like *Under Goliath* (Peter Carter) that invite the reader to explore other landscapes, other emotional worlds and ways of life, a central emphasis should be placed on books that speak directly to their readers, and at the same time, introduce an unexpectedly fresh fictional method that would provoke more active participation from the reader, like the diary narration in *Flowers for Algernon* (Daniel Keyes), *Z for Zachariah* (Robert C. O'Brien), and the letter story form of *Computers Don't Argue* (Gordon Dickson) and 'Too many funerals', David McRobbie (from *The Blue Storyhouse*).

There is a hint that their images of themselves as readers have changed through this approach to Fisk and Cormier from 'just reading it ... and the story just goes on from there' to images of themselves as productive initiators who bring meaning with them to the text. As Frank Kermode shrewdly remarks, 'The reader is not offered easy satisfactions, but a challenge to creative cooperation.'[2] It is this sense of an active challenge that the pupils register as well ('... all through this book you were working at it ... trying to think of the ending...' and 'but this story doesn't just unfold/You have to unfold it yourself'). More searching reading strategies are being demanded of them in making sense of the structural breaks and gaps in the text and there is evidence that they are on the way to developing into more competent readers.

The other main gain leads us on to the pupils' writing. The pupils not only make their own meanings from the story but have become more consciously aware of the composing process of the writer so that they can now say, 'I've certainly learnt a new way of writing (stories)...'. And the teacher's role in all this – laying bare something of the structural bones of story-making – is obviously crucial.

I want now to focus on the writing of one member of the group to see how this process of reading affected her decisions as a writer of stories. She took on the non-linear story form, tried to adapt it to her own interests and then commented on the problems of writing it like that. Here it is:

My attempt at being a cheese: (A novel)
When the news came through, it wasn't that much of a shock to any of us really, but anyway, it moved us into action. Let me explain. I'm a paratrooper and with all this palava over the Falklands, it was almost inevitable that I would be on the first ship that went. We said our farewells and that, but I know it sounds morbid, but I was quite looking forward to it. Action, I mean.

*   *   *   *

Why is war so cruel and unjust? Answer me that. A peace loving nation we call ourselves, but still we must fight. I dislike any violence so my friends call me a coward, but they are too stupid to understand. Conscription caught me out. Three years at College gone in the wind. Well, someone has to go but I find the idea of killing, nauseating.

*   *   *   *

During the first couple of days, they had us cleaning our rifles but we all got fed up with that, so we went to the Cap. to see what could be done, knew he'd rustle us up something. Today, we're doing keep fit on deck. At this rate, we'll all be too tired to fight but if I look on the bright side, the grub's fantastic. Chips and lovely rice pudding yesterday, better than me Mam. Sometimes I get restless with all this waiting. I just want to get there and fight.

*   *   *   *

So I got shipped onto the Island along with my troops to fight for our alleged country. Half of us, me included, aren't trained properly so I'd be useless in an emergency. On the island, it is so cold and most of us only have thin cotton jackets. And the food, we hardly see any, and when we do it's a meal big enough for only a bird!! Well enough complaining. Everyday we run round the island to keep in shape. Tomorrow, we are going to the other camp on South Falkland. This is something I hate to do. The armament hut is dismantled along with the cannons, bazookas and mortars. As well as these, there will be about 100 automatics plus 10,000 rounds of ammunition. I hate to see all these implementers of destruction around me, let alone actually use them.

*   *   *   *

The sarge says we're about 200 miles off the coast of South Falkland. Just wait 'til I get my hands on one of those guns. I'll kill every bloomin' Argentinian to hell. The fascists get right up my nose. Peace loving nation they call themselves. My Aunt Fanny! All of them are just waiting to kill us just like we are them. Maggie was right in sending us over here. the only way to get them out of our Islands is to blow 'em off!!!

*   *   *   *

Both the Argentinian and the British media covered the Falklands take over in different ways. The British taking the stance that everything they did was right and needed no justification while the Argentinians were the aggressors and assumed that anything the British did was wrong. As so the war progressed. The governments never coming to an agreement or compromise. The two soldiers in point both took different stances as well. The Britisher volunteering to go and the Argentinian made to. Their thoughts on the war are different. They survive in different surroundings and come from different families and countries.

※　　　※　　　※　　　※

As the dawn broke, The Argentinians patrol group already on South Falkland moved their base camp. They worked until dusk without rest or food. All of them were about falling down on the job but the heartless captain made them do an hours exercise. After that they all fell on the spot, exhausted.

About this time the Birmingham ship came within sight of South Falkland. All aboard were nervous at the sight of land. Men began to get their gear together with various guns and ammunition. Corporal Williams was quietly confident. He liked the prospect of fighting and bloodshed. He enjoyed pain and suffering. It could be said that he was a sadist. As the ship opened its paratrooper doors and the first glimpse of light came through. Last minute nerves got lost in the rush of bodies rushing out through the door.

※　　　※　　　※　　　※

The lookout spotted the ship a mile off the coast. He sounded the horn and woke the group. Within seconds the patrol was in position.

※　　　※　　　※　　　※

Nobody saw the Argentinians as they ran out. Corporal Williams caught sight of a pair of eyes and they caught sight of him. They raised their guns. And in that second, that split second, both were afraid, even Williams, with his nerves of steel; the Argentinian who was terrified of killing.

And then, and then, and then they blew each others brains out!!!

Comments
The first hurdle was trying to get the contrast of ideas. I thought my story was a bit predictable so I had to make the points of view very different. I think this whole Falklands business is blown out of proportion and could be solved in some other way, so I tried to put my thoughts into one of the soldiers (no, not the Britisher).

The next one was trying to get as much out of the soldiers as I could. Building on little things and advancing on them. All the time I had the ending in mind and so I tried to bring them together in subtle ways. Both characters were different but brought together by war, one wanted to kill and one didn't. I wanted to bring out the badness in one, the British, and the good in the Argentinian (a sort of role reversal). Writing this way, thinking about it, is probably one of the hardest things I've done. I picked up things from the papers and TV and exaggerated them. The fat Brit. with everything he wants and the skinny Argentine with a thin cotton jacket. That's about all really but maybe something else will crop up!!

Lindsay encounters the problems of an inexperienced writer trying out a difficult new form for the first time. She has learnt from the previous examples of 'taking two different stories at once' and handles the contrasted points of view of the British and Argentinian soldiers quite effectively. She manages to establish the brutalized, colloquial, down-to-earth tone of the British soldier ('The fascists get right up my nose. Peace loving nation they call themselves. My Aunt Fanny! All of them are just waiting to kill us just like we are them. Maggie was right in sending us over here. The only way to get them out of our Islands is to blow 'em off!!!') and puts it against the sensitively introspective voice of the Argentinian with sharp effect.

But her difficulties really begin with the section that starts, 'Both the Argentinian and the British media...' which is experienced by the reader as an awkward intrusion in the development of the 'contrast of ideas'. Her problem arises from the constraints imposed on her by having both the British and Argentinian soldiers use a first person perspective. She is trying to break out of the imprisonment of that kind of focus (finding that certain things cannot be said in that way) to gain a more distanced, generalized viewpoint. But the transition from the rest of the story to a more detached, third person narration (starting from 'As the dawn broke...') is gawkily botched.

The teacher comments in Lindsay's exercise book as she tries to help her through this stage of the story:

> What I wonder about is the storyline and that's why I imagine you are having difficulties – how to carry it on and be interesting and how to end it satisfactorily. Maybe it's not helped by the fact that here you've got two men to speak as 'I'. What about telling a story about them and their ideas and thoughts. Then the *story* can connect the two soldiers. At the moment they're so separate how can the two different areas come together? It's a difficult piece of writing to do – you've chosen a difficult theme – but keep trying.

Perhaps Lindsay can only deal with these problems properly when she gains more conscious control of how point of view is inextricably linked to choices about varying degrees of abstraction but at least she is on the way to seeing that these formal decisions and possibilities exist, in the first place.

Her comments on the process of writing the story show how explicitly aware she is becoming of the mechanics of story-making: 'The first hurdle was trying to get the contrast of ideas. I thought my story was a bit predictable so I had to make the points of view very different' and 'All the time I had the ending in my mind and so I tried to bring them together in subtle ways.' These crafting choices are not just isolated technical ones either; in the process of making decisions about the form of the story Lindsay is involved in having to sort out her own moral position about the Falkland Islands War through judgements about character portrayal and point of view: 'I think this whole Falklands business is blown out of proportion and could be solved in some other way, so I tried to put my thoughts into one of the soldiers (no, not the Britisher)' and 'I wanted to bring out the badness in one, the British, and the good in the Argentinian (a sort of role reversal) ... The fat Brit. with everything he wants and the skinny Argentine with a thin cotton jacket.'

In needing to question nationalistic, conditioning processes and point towards 'some other way' of solving the crisis Lindsay makes use of a fictional technique that will do justice to those perceptions. So her deliberate reversal of patriotic expectations ('no, not the Britisher') and her calculated use of a more subtle point of view contrast ('I thought my story was a bit predictable so I had to make the points of view very different') show her in the act of building up a more complex representation of the world as she begins to try out for herself an expanded sense of form.

This matching up of new forms with developing intentions is at the heart of extending the pupils' range as readers and writers in this difficult second phase. (And much can be learnt about those emerging pupil intentions through casual classroom gossip and the more regular exchanges of work diaries and journals.) And the teacher's role in all this is crucial. In their selection and organization of classroom resources and the building up of a constructive context for learning teachers can play a major role in widening out the pupils repertoire of possible forms, or as Margaret Donaldson puts it: 'As children master new literary forms in their reading, and so expand their resources as writers, teachers should take every opportunity of encouraging them to link the two activities in a consciously productive way.[3]

Other worlds, viewpoints, ways of living

There is a need at the upper-second-year/third-year stage for children to be encouraged to move out from an often narrowly circumscribed social experience and reading background to try out fictions that investigate other cultural landscapes, other emotional worlds, perspectives, and ways of living. Of course, in some ways, literature is always doing this – offering alternative, 'virtual' experiences as a change from the routine familiarities of the actual world but here, in this second phase of development, I would suggest that this approach can give an organizing direction to the way we shape the reading curriculum.

As well as being helped to take on new forms, techniques and styles in their reading, children need to encounter fictions that might extend the complexity of their views of themselves and the outside world. I use 'might' here because of the subtlety of the issue. Nicholas Tucker argues that, 'even though readers may be enabled in their imagination to step outside the historical, geographic and social boundaries that normally tie them down to the here and now, it could still be argued, ... that individuals will always respond to new imaginative experiences according to their already habitual psychological processes and defences'.[4] And he is right in so far as every child, in making sense of a fresh imaginative experience, has to be able to relate the new experience to what she already knows but, if chosen well, there are books available for children about the ages of 13 and 14 that set out to challenge and question the reader's habitual frame of values and cultural reference points and do seem to make significant impressions on some readers. Books like *It's My Life* (Robert Leeson), *The Basketball Game* (Julius Lester), some of the short stories in *A Sense of Shame and Other Stories* (Jan Needle), such as 'The common good'. But for our purposes here I want to concentrate on just one – *Under Goliath* (Peter Carter).

UNDER GOLIATH

Belfast, where the book is set, is a disturbingly familiar and yet totally unknown landscape for the average British person. It is familiar in a superficial sense because Belfast's communities – Shankill, Falls, Crumlin, Ardoyne – have flickered through our consciousness over the last thirteen years from the media but, in a deeper sense, Belfast is a guilty secret, strange and unknown in its savagely intense hatreds. So all the more reason for introducing into English classrooms books that offer more fully developed, mature perspectives on neglected but important backgrounds.

Placed in the Belfast of 1969 at the start of the Civil Rights' marches and the ensuing troubles, *Under Goliath* deals with 13-year-old Alan Kenton's life in a Protestant family, his failed attempt to maintain a friendship with a Catholic boy called Fergus Riley, and his growing understanding of sectarian divisions and prejudice that corrupt everything with which they come into contact (and most importantly for him his relationship with Fergus).

The representative importance of the book for its use, say, in the middle or towards the end of the third year, is that it invites the reader to get inside the skin of apparently alien ways of living and to develop an understanding of different ways of thinking and the reasons for people being the way they are. At a time when many children only hear garbled rumours about what is happening in Northern Ireland and see an often trivialized view of things from without, it is valuable to be able to take up a much more informed and complex vantage point. Indeed the whole book is dedicated to this gradual increase in empathy:

> I saw a beast upon a mountain side.
> It came closer and I saw it was a man.
> We drew together, and it was my brother.

> Persian proverb

At the start of the book we see Alan as an uncritical part of the rival systems of bigotry and prejudice operating in Northern Ireland. He joins an Orange Lodge walking band because he wants to play the drum, and merely obeys his Uncle Jack's suggestion to jeer and blow a raspberry at a Catholic piper boy. He is just unthinkingly slotting into the automatic routine of fear and superstition that keeps the Catholic and Protestant communities so far apart. This fear of the unknown magnifies the Catholic Piper into a nightmarish shape in Alan's eyes:

> As I plodded up the street the Piper didn't move. His head was turned towards me but his cap shaded it and it was as if he was wearing a mask. That frightened me as much as the thought of a hammering from the Piper's fists. At school once Mr Craigie said that everyone is frightened of the unknown, and I did not know what expression was on the Piper's face. But more than that, he was a Catholic, and that was the greatest unknown of all.
>
> That might seem an amazing thing to say when you think that I lived in a country of one and a half million, and that nearly a third of them were Catholics, but it's true.... All the Catholics I know were either grown up or kids. The lads my age seemed to disappear. They went to different schools, different clubs, different bands, and a different church.
>
> And that was the heart of the matter. Even the Catholic families I did know were wrapped up in religion in a way I didn't understand. It had something to do with bleeding hearts and plaster statues; mumbling in a foreign language, having the priest round telling you what to do...

Through a scrambled fight, where they are both able to rid themselves to some extent of the irrational fears of the other person, the shadowy Piper becomes a real person to Alan – Fergus Riley. They also find a new kind of companionship by finding a buried gun in the boarded up house they use as a place to fight in ('... a secret shared with the laddie I had thought a deadly enemy...').

Bob Dixon[5] is right in feeling that the relationship is a bit undermotivated but nevertheless the overall impression of the development within their relationship is convincing. A simplistic, sectarian view of the world is replaced in Alan by a more puzzlingly complex one: 'The band played, you played. The band marched, you marched. The Protestants marched, the Catholics marched, you saw them and they saw you.... It was all very simple, except it was beginning to seem a bit more complicated to me.'

Alan is now able to question some of the habitual assumptions behind the fixed, hostile attitudes of both sides and, helped by his brother Billy, see the common, economic and social realities that directly affect *both* Protestants and Catholics. ('[Fergus] was just a Belfast lad, his dad had been in the army, he lived in a street like mine...'.)

If the story had just stopped there it would have been too neatly schematic. What gives the story more subtlety and density is the way the main metaphorical energies of the book (the images of the gun and the drum) are used by the writer to establish an historical context that frames and limits the impulses being generated within the personal relationships.

The gun, with its threatening, malevolent presence, carrying with it its memories of past sectarian violence and the most recent troubles of 1924 and 1951, seems to constrain the independent actions of both boys: 'It was as if the gun was telling us what to do...'. The gun is associated with all those old, festering grievances and frozen attitudes – the spirit of people like Uncle Jack, Mackracken and Mr Riley – that re-opened in 1969 with the Civil Rights' marches and coincided with the gun being brought back into the light, 'like something that had been buried for a long time'. It is these buried systems of hate, fear and suspicion, re-activated by the new troubles, that come between the boys.

Too late they try to get rid of the gun, but it has been taken by somebody else to use in the present violence. They are left, with the old fears and anxieties returned, to destroy their relationship in a suspicious row that ends with Alan consumed by the 'burning on my cheek and the bitter rage in my heart'. Later Fergus saves Alan from the worst street riot, and there is a brief moment of reconciliation and understanding but the enduring impression, underlined by the structure of the Prologue and Epilogue, is the 'writer's rage at borders without meaning except that they divide the hearts of men'.

The drum image increases the contradictoriness of Alan's position and makes his growth of understanding more credible. The great, swaggering sectarian pride of the street band, and particularly the effect of the drum, cries out to Protestants, 'You're the cocks of the walk alright. You're the ones round here who've got the shout', and what is convincing is that Alan learns to understand the band's significance in those systems of hatred but can also experience its hypnotic power as well.

> And the lambeg spoke. Boom Boom Boom. Boom Boom Boom. Boom Boom Boom! In the yard, surrounded by brick walls, the great voice of the lambeg swirled and echoed, seeming to make the air thicken and then to make that thickness boil, like molten iron.... And I hoped that over there, in those other streets, there where the bagpipes wailed, I hoped that there the people heard us, yes, and not only heard us but trembled as they did so. Yes, even Riley.

Temporarily Alan is prepared to allow the old, mad forces of habit and instinctive reaction to work on him through the power of the band and drum ('They carried you along, sucking you behind them so that the faces of the crowd became a blur...') as he purges himself of his destructive feelings, gained since the argument, towards Fergus. But his new, more rational understandings of the common position of both Catholics and Protestants win out in the end. He gives up the band and he turns to pigeons.

A story like *Under Goliath* can help to introduce pupils to new territories and landscapes of entangled feeling and thinking where, in order to cope, they have to look at experience through the unfamiliar eyes of an Alan or a Fergus, and perhaps by so doing they might gather into their customary worldviews other people's ways of looking at themselves and the world. Of course we can never be sure about the exact connections between these fresh reading experiences and our pupils' habitual perceptions in everyday life, but it does seem worthwhile in providing for their searching inquisitiveness about other people, in other land-scapes. They do not like stagnating or going over the same kind of ground in their reading habits and the more we cater for an increasing complexity in their tastes and worldview the more likely we are to absorb them in reading fiction.

Using multi-racial stories in an all-white school

All-white schools often breed warped attitudes towards race. Excluded from daily, multi-racial encounters and exchanges such schools often find it extremely difficult to encourage in their pupils any real respect for racial diversity. Experiences like the one that occurred in my presence on a recent coach trip for first formers where a 12-year-old girl stood up and shouted, 'There's a wog!' as we were passing through a neighbouring town, are fairly common.

Chatting about this difficulty with a group of 14-year-olds the pupils commented to me:

> *Tim* We don't know much about that kind of thing (multi-racial issues) ... this problem ... because it doesn't happen very much at this school...
>
> *Wendy* No one here really lives in a really run down kind of place like some coloured people live in ... people automatically say coloured people live in

> run-down places and white people live in posh
> houses ... but it's not necessarily true ... some
> coloured people really get along well with every-
> body else ... but some go out of their way to be
> horrible and cause aggro ... and you brand them
> and you brand everybody else ... by their colour.
>
> *Teacher* So what can books do about that?
>
> *Paula* Books can separate them ... that everybody isn't
> the same ... and have two black people completely
> different ... and one getting on with the white
> person and one not...

Stories can play a small but significant part, as one of the
many shaping influences on children's attitudes towards race,
in helping pupils to move away from these automatic,
branding habits of thought, that Wendy talks about, towards
the building up of a more complex and understanding
worldview.

All through the secondary school children need a regular
opportunity and positive encouragement to read, listen and
talk about stories that offer views of the world through the
eyes of various ethnic minorities and this should be evident in
the books we select in reading suggestions' lists, class
libraries, school bookshop and library and the main English
stock. But this priority is particularly important in the second
phase's stress on the need to expand pupil perspective.

In *Reading and Race*[6] Michael Simons and Paul Ashton (in
referring to Sara Zimet's book, *Print and Prejudice*) stress two
main points about classroom treatment of stories that deal
with multi-racial issues. 'A coherent series of lessons has more
impact on attitude than one-off lessons', and that often a
chance to explore their reading together in small groups often
encourages a more mature expression of attitudes rather than
the unthinking slogans of large, whole group discussion. So,
bearing this in mind, I took up a month's (four) class library
reading lessons to introduce some of the short stories of

Farrukh Dhondy in *Come to Mecca* and Samuel Selvon in *Ways of Sunlight* with a small group of four third-year pupils. For the purposes of a necessarily limited investigation I want to concentrate on the pupils' responses to one of the stories in *Come to Mecca*, called 'Free dinners'.

'Free dinners' is seen through the eyes of a white working-class boy called Peter, and involves the developing relationship between him and Lorraine, a half-caste black girl from the first year at secondary school to working in the outside world. At the start of secondary school they are both humiliated by having to have free dinners. But whereas Lorraine does not seem to take any notice Peter has to hide his shame by retreating to the toilets.

Later on in school Lorraine starts to stick up for herself and becomes openly resistant to authority (and especially to the school deputy head) when she turns up to a school prize giving wearing velvet hot-pants and crimson lipstick, and then later spits in the deputy head's coffee cup.

Although Peter is going out with Wendy, he is intrigued by Lorraine and eventually asks her out. Peter's racism and prejudice is shown by a trip to a Chinese restaurant and later in a sixth-form discussion group.

After leaving school Peter becomes an apprentice architect and starts to become more aware as he meets up with Lorraine, first as an ineffectual pub stripper, and then as a prostitute getting a 'free dinner' out of a customer.

One of the immediate problems is that unless there is a consistently positive support from a whole school policy or from an active teacher, the pupils will just ignore certain collections of multi-racial stories on the shelves (two copies of *Come to Mecca* in the school library have never been taken out in the six months they have been there), or retreat behind a front of indifference ('it's got nothing to do with me') on meeting cultural backgrounds of initial strangeness.

Certainly that is what some members of this group of third-

formers felt on encountering Lorraine's aggressive resistance
for the first time:

Teacher What's the difference between the stories that you
normally read and this story?

Wendy ... the ones that we normally read are characters
that you can imagine ... schoolgirls ... I know this
one's about schoolgirls ... but it had bits in where
you thought, 'Oh I didn't think she'd do that' or 'I
didn't think he'd do something like that'...

Teacher Which bits in particular?

Wendy ... the bit where she came in in black velvet hot
pants ... and when she spat in the tea...

Teacher Did you find that a bit difficult to accept then?

Tim Yea ... I don't know why she did it...

Wendy's habitual cultural preconceptions, shaped by the
social and economic context of living where she does, make it
difficult for her to relate what she already knows ('...
characters that you can imagine' meaning mostly well-
behaved schoolgirls) to the abrasive rebelliousness of Lorraine
in 'Free dinners' so that she can take it on in her own terms.
For Tim, lacking a wide enough social and political understanding, Lorraine's actions just seem arbitrarily wilful. And
at this precarious stage of reading many children in all-white
schools turn away from stories that make them feel uncom-
fortable, bewildered, or are too far removed from their usual
ways of making sense. Unless, that is, the strength of the
writing still keeps them engrossed in the story.[7] The whole
framework of institutional humiliation is revealed so power-
fully by Farrukh Dhondy, as in moments where the deputy
head instructs the girl prize winners not to wear any '... blue
and green tights. I want all the girls to wear flesh-coloured
tights'. 'Whose flesh, miss?' Lorraine asks. And the writing in
the Chinese restaurant and pub scenes is so physically direct
that the pupils' curiosities are partly hooked, even though
there are still moments of blank incomprehension.

These genuine curiosities about race and other social backgrounds can lead on, with teacher support, to a more explicit awareness of how these limiting cultural assumptions are constructed and how they can get in the way of the reader who wants to get on the inside of a different way of thinking and of seeing the world:

T.　What do you think the problems are about living in Bingham in understanding other ways of living?

W.　There aren't many ... different races of people here so we don't really get the chance to mix with them.

S.　When you read these books it widens your range ... and how you can write stories ... if you don't read through books that are different ... all your work will be the same.

W.　If we didn't read books like that we'd all get the idea that all coloured people are hated by white people ... and all coloured people do this, that and the other.

T.　Where would you pick that up from then?

P.　Well television programmes ... they have programmes on the Brixton riots and it's about people who started it ... and you read a book like this ... and it changes your way of thinking about it ... it helps you to understand it better.

T.　What are the dangers of this kind of approach?

Tim　I think a lot of people ... if they read that book would say, 'Oh blooming niggers' ... whip 'em and come out with something like that.

T.　Why?

Tim　I don't know ... just to make people think they're big and hard ... and they can complain against this and they're not serious about it.

P.　Course if somebody hates black people ... then whoever they go round with hates them ... they follow the leader.

W.　I was with a lad and he goes, 'Oh d'you like black

> people?' and he says 'Ohh!' ... he just walked away
> ... and wouldn't talk to me anymore...
>
> T. You mean just keeping in with a gang opinion ...
> how can books do anything about that?
>
> W. Well they can't change some people ... some people
> are really set ... 'Oh I don't like black people'.
>
> P. Yea but they're not the sort who read books anyway.
>
> T. They just come to an English lesson ... turn off ... go
> to sleep for an hour...
>
> W. Nobody'd be reading books like *Roots* or whatever it
> is ... about the black people being made slaves ... yea
> ... I don't think they choose books like that to read.

Although there are teacher-approved answers here the
pupils are edging their way towards working out their own
wider frame of social reference for the story; so that they are
seen in the process of understanding how the media can
reinforce automatic blanket judgements about race ('... all
coloured people do this, that and the other...') and that the
pressure of peer group approval can move certain pupils
towards passive, racist conformity. They appreciate that
stories can't 'change some people ... some people are really
set...' but some stories, if they're good enough, can begin to
challenge ingrained, stereotyped attitudes and ways of
thinking.

Later, the group was able to talk itself into a more informed
position, but not without difficulty. Never having been
exposed to such a persistent battery of affronts to their
personal dignity, like Lorraine in that particular context, they
are still having problems in seeing through to the causes and
reasons behind Lorraine's apparently outrageous behaviour:

> W. I can understand that (Lorraine) gets mad at what
> white people say ... they try to talk like her ... they're
> really horrible to her ... I'd get mad ... but some of
> the things ... I don't think she had any cause to spit in
> that cup ... I don't see what she did that for?

Tim The teacher never did anything against her personally
    ... probably ...
T.   Why do you think she needed to do that?
W.   To prove to the class that she's a hardo ... don't do
      anything wrong to her or she'll whack you one.
S.   She probably just wants to be noticed ... as some-
      body special ... wants attention.
W.   She just wants attention...

Even though Wendy is starting to put herself into Lorraine's position emotionally, the group is still construing her
actions in too restricted and individualist a way. Tim lacks the
ability to connect up the local details of the story ('... the
teacher never did anything against her personally ... probably ...') with a more far-reaching social frame of reference
and explanation. The teacher (the deputy-head) is a part of a
network of control and power within the school that reduces
Lorraine's worth and makes her feel invisible. That is why she
turns up in hot pants and crimson lipstick and gets her own
back on the deputy head by spitting in her cup. Lorraine
might have felt against her personally but also as an inextric-
able part of a racist society that is denying her own
independent identity.

Real understanding of the emotional springs of Lorraine's
actions comes through Wendy turning the tables on herself.
She imaginatively possesses the spirit of 'Free dinners' by
speculating on her own possible reactions as 'the only white
kid in a black school':

W. The thing is people don't really think of blacks being
   really good ... I know some of them are but you see the
   Brixton riots ... you see those and you think ... all
   them ... they're not exactly being angelic are they?
   chucking stones at people...
T. Do you think stories can do anything about this?
W. They make you see why they feel that way ... why they
   do act like that ... because I think if I was the only

white kid in a black school ... and everybody started teasing me about being white ... saying I didn't fit in and everything ... I'd feel really mad and think I'd do things that I didn't really mean to do just to prove to them that it's not so bad being white ... I could do better than them even though I am white...

T. You might even spit in your teacher's cup?

W. Yea!

Although some members of the group, like Tim, are left outside the central experience of the story because of limiting preconceptions, Wendy is able, through the gradual penetration of the talk, to find correspondences of feeling between Lorraine and herself and, momentarily, to stand in another vantage point and try out the world through somebody else's eyes. 'I'd feel really mad and I think I'd do things that I didn't really mean to do ...'.

Some stories, like 'Free dinners', with enough strength and vitality in their telling, can motivate some sheltered readers to 'see why the characters in stories feel that way', and 'why they act like that', given a teacher who is prepared to provide enough time for pupils to talk their way into the main currents of feeling within the story. And as such, experiences like this, although apparently minor in their own way, can join up with other constructive forces in helping pupils to cut their way through the automatic 'branding' of people seen in some of the worst banner headlines (as in the *Daily Telegraph* description of the Brixton disturbances – 'LOOTING GANGS ROAM BRIXTON/TEENAGE MOBS POUR OUT TO BOMBARD POLICE', 13 April, 1981) and the most negative and prejudiced television programmes.

Notes

1 'Building up a part: Laughton's Galileo' included in the notes on *The Life of Galileo*, ed. John Willett and Ralph

Mannheim, London, Eyre Methuen, 1980.

2 Frank Kermode, *The Sense of an Ending*, London, Oxford University Press, 1969.

3 From 'Literature and language development', in *Children, Language and Literature*, Milton Keynes, Open University, Department of Continuing Education, 1982.

4 Nicholas Tucker, *The Child and the Book*, Cambridge University Press, 1981.

5 *Now Read On – Recommended Fiction for Young People*, London, Pluto Press, 1982.

6 Included in *Children, Language and Literature*.

7 Consider in this context a revealing contrast in the quality of the writing between two books of multi-racial fiction. Whereas attempts to confirm and respect racial diversity come *through* the power of the writing in such scenes as 'Integrating the white library' from *The Basketball Game* (Julius Lester), scenes like Becky and Candy encountering the policeman in the park included in *Go Well, Stay Well* (Toecky Jones) seem in contrast to be artificially worked up to get a message over.

8
THIRD PHASE:
REFLECTIVE AWARENESS
14–16+

Dealing with a set book in literature at 16+: *Great Expectations* (Charles Dickens)

At times I catch myself blasting off about the special advantages of not having a specific body of knowledge in English teaching. But I have only got to dredge up what I was doing in English literature classes a few years ago, and that still partly shapes what I do now, to realize that's far from the case.

You will probably recognize the scene (fill in the gaps for yourself). The desks are all turned to the front. Almost all the pupils have their heads down and are furiously scribbling away. It is the run in to the examination time and my anxiety about their possible results has pushed me, yet again, into giving them notes on the main themes and characters. There is some thoughtful discussion about several points but it is always the same few, active members of the group who take part.

My notes come from remembered enthusiasms and insights about *Great Expectations* gained from reading it again during the holiday before this present group's literature course began. Atmospheres from the book – the bleak marshland of Pip's 'oppressed conscience', Miss Havisham ('... waxwork and skeleton seemed to have dark eyes that moved and looked at me'), the magnificent river – Chapter 54 – still haunt me, but close reading techniques, gathered from habits of practical criticism picked up in my training, are tending to harden out into mechanical, routine procedures. So that even before I hear what the pupils make of the book I have already filled an A4 sheet of paper (to help me to make detailed references to the book later when my memory of particular episodes is fading) with precise references to themes, characters and language, such as:

> *Pip* – fertile imagination, page 41*; guilty conscience, 44; imaginative empathy with the convict, 45; awakened moral sympathy, 48; stifling of spontaneity by Mrs Joe, 54; Mrs Joe's starchiness, 57; tenderness for Joe, 78.[1]

My attitudes and approaches to the book are already setting fast like concrete even before I walk into the first literature class. So here in this detailed evidence and concreted attitudes are some of the main English teacher's blocks of knowledge and the problem is that they often get in the way of pupils' understanding at 16+.

SPOON FEEDING

Our personal insights into what we read as teachers can help the pupils when they feel confirmed in their responses but, often, they are too easily impressed or intimidated by them. And there are far worse tendencies to be found in the traditional examination course on literature: 'A fifth year group in English had written 23,000 words of dictated plot of

Far from the Madding Crowd, and would have written many more when they had finished *Great Expectations* already under way' (from *Aspects of Secondary Education*, London, HMSO, 1981).

Reading experiences are often reduced to filing cabinets of factual information. And pupils are drilled and rehearsed in memory tests and efficient examination packaging skills.

As a result questioning pupils get the feeling that they are being spoon fed. They are being told what to think and feel about books they read by people like me with my notes on Pip's character. And that kind of teacher-telling, or more subtle nudging, usually ends up with the pupils re-telling like parrots, without ever having had the chance to go through processes of understanding that might have made the book more real to them.

So how do we move out of this dead end?

MAKING IT YOUR OWN

Real learning means making knowledge personal. .... This is only possible when we express the new experience (in this instance the experience of reading *Great Expectations*) in our own language in our own way . . .' (Harold Rosen, from The Language of Text Books: *Language in Education*, London, Routledge, 1972.)

Pupils only begin to make a reading experience their own by using talk and provisional jotting as ways of fitting that new and unfamiliar experience into their already existing systems of understanding.

Here I want to look closely at some fresh ways[2] of getting out of the dictated notes trap and how they help the pupil to come at stories, poems and plays through a series of preliminary learning stages that probably give her a more effective way of possessing for herself the special qualities of those reading experiences.

The pupils are from a nine-form entry mixed comprehensive school in Nottinghamshire. They have all opted to do the Cambridge Plain Texts O-level English Literature course offered within a fourth- and fifth-year option choice operated from within the English department. Some of the pupils' work shown below is from the last term in the fourth year and the first two terms of the fifth year. The set book, *Great Expectations*, could be taken into the final exam.

JOTTING DOWN FIRST IMPRESSIONS (THE FIRST NINE CHAPTERS)

This kind of rough jottings is not as easy to get from pupils as it looks, particularly if you are starting from cold in the fifth year. The pupils need to be trained up, from early days, to take on such an approach. As the work on reading journals (see above) shows, if carefully introduced and properly organized, children can be weaned onto the regular habits of detailed observation that this approach needs if it is to be done effectively. But adequate preparation is necessary. (See 'Keeping a reading log or journal to act as a running commentary on what you read', and the worksheet that Donald Fry gives out to his pupils to explain a reading log approach that is included in his chapter 'Reflecting on English: keeping work diaries', in Mike Torbe (ed.), *Language, Teaching and Learning*, vol. 3: *English* (London, Ward Lock Educational, 1981.)

The warmth, concern and tentativeness of the teacher's response to these pupil jottings is probably the crucial factor in all this. Teacher remarks like, 'I've always meant to read *I Am David* because several people have recommended it...' and 'Come and chat to me about reading books...' establish a tone of relaxed vulnerability that supports pupils to feel more confident in admitting uncertainties and blockages. This is the kind of background context within which one fifth-year pupil produced a series of rough jottings on the first nine chapters of *Great Expectations*:

Chapter

1st 1st page – horrible style. Difficult to make sense of, needs reading twice.
Description of convict – excellent. Very lucid. Who is convict? Where is story going?

2nd Mrs Joe – v. good descriptive – readable, and amusing in places.
Description of Pip's guilty conscience at having to steal is beautiful. Vocabulary is awkward and book doesn't seem to know where it's going.

3rd 1st paragraph ('it was a rimy morning and very damp') is superb. So is story of journey through the mist.

4th Analogies very illogical ('. . . be as to our fingers, like monumented Crusaders is to the legs').
Style is getting easier, but book is at odds with itself. What is it doing?

5th Soldiers? Confusing. Story of chase after convicts good but what is happening?
The author's strength seems to be his powers of description.
The style is awkward – dozens of commas to the sentence.
The plot seems bitty, but I'll give it a chance.

6th Another complete change of tack. I'm having problems remembering what's going on. Might get easier as I get used to the style.

7th 2nd para. a gem. Joe explaining his life looks like an end to the whole episode. Is the book now going to jump a year or two? No. What has Miss Havisham got to do with the convict?
V. odd.

8th Apparently a turning point. Is Pip being sent to Miss H's permanently?

Finally, author is beginning to prognosticate as well as describe.

Many unanswered questions about Miss H.

Pip is timid, weak, easily influenced.

Pip is ashamed, and ashamed of admitting it and ashamed of not admitting it.

This seems to be one shaping event in Pip's life. Is the book going to describe all the events of people that shaped Pip?

(DAVID BULL)

Here we find David gradually easing himself into the book and being able through the jottings, to find a place where he can own up to the *problems* of making sense for himself of what he's reading ('Difficult to make sense of, needs reading twice...') rather than borrowing the teacher's prefabricated phrases. Also the teacher is put into a much more useful position of being able to start from where the pupil actually is rather than where she would like David to be.

Through the initial strangeness of having to come to terms with an elaborated style that makes unfamiliar demands on him as a reader the book starts to open up for him: '3rd [chapter] 1st paragraph ('it was a rimy morning and very damp') is superb. So is story of journey through the mist.'

David is starting to express his own point of view in a series of speculations and puzzlings and is converting the experience of reading the book into his own terms. And, simultaneously, there's a sorting out and explanation going on. As another member of the group said in answer to the question 'Did the first impressions jotting in your journals help you to understand the book?'. 'Writing things down helps you get your thoughts straight in your mind. If you write out your thoughts, your feelings become clearer. Also, if you have two points of view you can argue them out reasonably on paper.'

The act of getting a dimly understood thought out of the head and down on paper helps David to clarify his reactions to the book.

The main clarification going on in David's first impressions is his attempt to find an underlying structure in the book. Frequently he questions its apparently random patchiness ('... book doesn't seem to know where it's going...'/'... the book is at odds with itself.../'... the plot seems bitty...') and seems frustrated by the tacking turns of the plot. What this preliminary jotting is allowing David to do is to bring in his expectations as a part of his general search for a whole meaning in what he's reading. (In this connection see the points made in *Prediction* and *The Turbulent Term of Tyke Tiler*, a sub-section of 'Learning to become an active reader', for a detailed classroom way of recognizing and using pupil expectation as a part of reading for meaning.) So his anticipation of some kind of structural coherence (i.e. that the book is not a collection of isolated descriptive pieces) is one of the main reasons why he's offended by the 'bittiness' as he sees it.

The book becomes clearer to David at the point where he is able to make out an organizing principle and a connection between local description and future action ('Finally, author is beginning to prognosticate as well as describe.'). He sees that the thing that holds all this detail together is the shaping influence on Pip: 'Is the book going to describe all the events of people that shaped Pip?'

At this stage he is starting to synthesize his disjointed reactions into a more organized system for understanding the book. And because of that he is able to see himself more completely as somebody capable of making his own meaning out of what he encounters.

PULLING THE IMPRESSIONS TOGETHER

Impressions and questionings within a single mind represent an important first step in response but they need to meet other views if they are going to gain a more fully developed and sharpened focus. Building up patterns of meaning together through small group talk, often away from the teacher domination of whole group exchanges, helps pupils to break out of an isolated commitment to a limited number of views to take on a much wider spread of alternative angles. Many of the group were struggling, like David, to make sense of *Great Expectations* and often lacked his staying power and logical grasp. So opportunities for swapping impressions, setting up a collective strength, through small group talk need to exist alongside the written jottings.

After this initial phase of confirming pupils' initiatives, of being able to make up their own minds from a position of relative power, teachers have a much better chance of exchanging views without their understandings muzzling the pupils' ones. Admittedly, it's difficult to stop yourself from blurting out your views but there are growing signs that more teachers are wanting to join in conversations, rather than instructional lectures with pupils, where the teacher's voice is not seen as the only approved way of reacting to the book. And, of course, a great deal depends on the pupils' habitual ways of coming at a book that have been laid down in the three years before.

Handled tactfully teachers have a crucial role at this point in helping to encourage faltering insights and assisting pupils to make their views more precisely explicit. Often the teacher still gets in the way but there are also more promising signs.

Let us have a look now at a transcript of an exchange between a teacher and three pupils.

(C = Caroline, B = Barbara, G = Gary and T = Teacher)

C. ... all through the book people are trying to get one up over everyone else ... and that it's about social climbing...

G. ... he was common first working with the blacksmith then he met Miss Havisham ... who was a snobbish person and he thought, 'I want to be like that so I can marry Estella'...

T. What about the ending of the story? Is Pip still snobbish?

G. Not really. I think he realizes what's been happening...

B. ...he realizes he's not so good to be at the top ... all the time ... and he realizes that it's best to be what he really was at the beginning...

T. How does he realize that?

C. ...well because when he was ill Joe came and sort of sat by him ... he was still loyal to him ... despite Pip not having spoken to him for ages...

T. Why does Pip feel sympathy for Magwitch out on the marshes?

C. ... because they both feel rejected ... the convict's rejected by society ... and Pip's rejected by his family ... everyone's always picking on him ... and everyone's always picking on the convict ... so he sees himself like the convict ... out on a limb

B. ... Pip's got no family ... or he's only got Joe to turn to ... whereas the convict's only got him to turn to ... he feels he can trust him ... because he's scared of him...

T. What are the things that Dickens is criticizing in the book?

C. ... people wanting to be what they're not...

T. Such as?

C. Oh well, Pip wanting to be a gentleman ... and I think maybe Estella wanting to pull him down all the time ... I think ... somewhere deep inside here ... she doesn't really want to do it.

G. I think that's maybe Miss Havisham's view ... she wants Estella to do that...

B. I think she was using Estella to do it wasn't she? Using Pip for her revenge on all men ... getting her to do it ... just because it happened to her ... she'd got to do it to somebody else ... as revenge ... and she'd picked on Estella to do it to Pip.

C. I also think Pumblechook & Wopsle are trying to be

> better than they are as well ... trying to be high
> society...
>
> B. Mrs Joe's like that ... she was just a blacksmith's wife
>   and yet she made herself feel more important than
>   anybody...

The teacher's intervention here is sometimes just an inter-
ruption to an emerging line of thought (as in the question
about the ending blocking off Gary's developing arc of
enquiry), but in other places it works as a supportive
framework within which the pupils can concentrate their
attention on what they have made of the book.

Frequently, these early jotted reactions seem sketchy,
disparate units of response and urgently need more time for a
more thorough pondering on. Through this sharing in talk
pupils can learn to stand back from the often impulsive over-
reaction of their first meeting and, although still remaining
loyal to the spirit of that first flavour, move towards a more
controlled, unified perspective. By pooling hunches and
exploring them more systematically they can often create their
own explanatory framework.

In the transcript, although they have not totally integrated
Magwitch into these frameworks (they can see there's a
correspondence between Pip and him '... out on a limb ...'
but they have not connected that with the structure of
inequality and privilege running through the novel), they are
defining some of the main strands of the book in their own
words: '... all through the book people are trying to get one
up over every one else ...'; '... he realizes that it's best to be
what he really was at the beginning ...' and '... people
wanting to be what they're not...'.

The pupils are talking themselves into a position where they
can understand the behaviour of Pip, Estella, Miss Havisham,
Pumblechook, Wopsle and Mrs Joe all through the unifying,
interpretative network of '... people want to be what they're
not...'.

So that later, they can come up with a more considered focus on the novel where personal feeling, intelligence and commentary all merge with one another. Here a 16-year-old pupil, half-way through the course, looks back in a more reflective way in her reading journal, after having been given the chance through small group discussion in class, to work out how she thinks Pip develops through the novel.

The change in (Pip) comes when he meets Miss Havisham and Estella. Estella made an impression on him, and you usually find that when someone admires someone else, they copy them. Pip realized that he wants to be posh and refined, like her. I think that meeting Miss H. and Estella was the worst thing that's happened to Pip. It made him ashamed of his home and background, and made him even more of an outcast. It made him want to achieve more than he is capable of. I don't think that he will become a gentleman, he hasn't the character to pull it through. He will be even more dissatisfied with his life – poor thing!

(CAROLINE FALCONER)

THINKING ABOUT THE BOOK THROUGH DIAGRAMS

Translating their thoughts into another medium often produces a valuable distancing effect that helps the pupils to organize their reactions to the book more closely and connectedly. As a fifth-former commented, 'It helped you sort out in your mind who was with who, and who wasn't.' Getting the story straight for themselves is the first part of this (and the interrelationship between characters) and then they can move on to systematizing their fragmentary response into patterns of meaning. This is a particularly important strategy to use when the teacher feels that the pupils, in their spoken and written reactions to a book, are tinkering away on the margins of the reading experience and need the incentive of a wider framework of reference in order to develop a more globally coherent approach where small, local details have to

(A)

Joe – Pip's only friend. Simple, innocent, honest and open. Also beaten by Mrs Joe. Still remained loyal despite Pip's selfishness.

Mrs Joe – brought Pip up by hand. Her beatings made Pip vulnerable and sensitive.

Trabbs Boy – showed Pip up for the snob he was. Because it was true it hurt Pip.

Orlicke – killed Mrs Joe – tried to kill Pip. Frightened him.

Pumblechook – made Pip feel guilty, because he kept saying how he should be grateful at being brought up by hand.

Biddy – sensible girl – liked Pip. He would have been better off with her.

PIP

Estella – proud, haughty, and pretty. Pip fell in love with her, but she snubbed him. She put him down, and made him ashamed of his home, made his expectations.

Wopsle – along with Pumblechook made Pip feel small, insignificant and guilty.

Herbert – was the pale young gentleman, and Pip's room mate. Both got into debt.

Magwitch – the convict who made an impression on Pip so early. Made Pip feel guilty all the time. Pip related to the convict He too was lonely and outcast. He provided Pip with his fortune, so made him the selfish dissatisfied person. But also made Pip change again when he came back into the country, and gave Pip someone to think about, other than himself.

Miss Havisham – weird old lady, with a fixation about the time before her wedding. Set to bring revenge on all men, with Estella. Introduced Pip to Estella, and so made him discontent.

be related to deeper structures of meaning. This, of course, might not happen but the attempt is worth making. (I always supply the pupils with examples of other spider plans – see the ones in 'Arguing with what you read' in the chapter 'Expanding approaches to reading' included in my *Continuity in Secondary English*, London, Methuen, 1982 – and other forms of diagrammatic representation that other classes have done when I am explaining what thinking through diagrams means.)

Diagram (A) shows Pip as the central consciousness of the book and is very useful in helping this fifth-former to map out more exactly the various shaping influences surrounding Pip, but it is a static model and does not really allow the pupil to express co-ordinated impressions or a sense of development in time through the novel.

Finding meaning in the book is often the same as gathering single and disparate clues together into a more unified network of significance. This is not easily learnt and what these diagrams do is to assist pupils to organize their meaning-making more precisely. Getting their half-formed ideas down on paper often puts pupils in a better position to reflect on and modify first impressions – and to create links between different moments, from a more detached position.

In (B) the organizing of meaning takes the form of a circle. The pupil explained why he'd done it like that:

> It seems to me that Pip's life forms a circle. He starts as a warm-hearted, human person, goes through various degrees of snobbery and comes back to being warm and human. Each person he meets moves him along one place round this circle. So it seems logical to set it out in this way.

There are misunderstandings here (like Herbert being a snob) but the pupil is finding his own way of bringing together the different parts of Pip's life. The circular structure keeps in closer tune with the movement of the book (unlike diagram (A)) and through the rise and fall contrast shows up the hollowness of those social snobbery aspirations at the

(B)

The meaning of the story

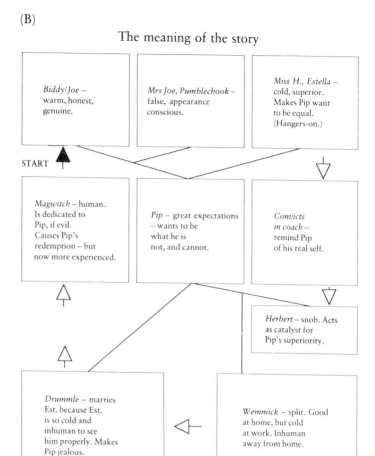

Biddy/Joe – warm, honest, genuine.

Mrs Joe, Pumblechook – false, appearance conscious.

Miss H., Estella – cold, superior. Makes Pip want to be equal. (Hangers-on.)

START

Magwitch – human. Is dedicated to Pip, if evil. Causes Pip's redemption – but now more experienced.

Pip – great expectations – wants to be what he is not, and cannot.

Convicts in coach – remind Pip of his real self.

Herbert – snob. Acts as catalyst for Pip's superiority.

Drummle – marries Est. because Est. is so cold and inhuman to see him properly. Makes Pip jealous.

Wemmick – split. Good at home, but cold at work. Inhuman away from home.

heart of the reading experience. Hence the balloon at the centre of the diagram. So that he links a moment like '"He calls the knaves, Jacks, this boy!" said Estella' with another at the very end of the book ('I opened my eyes in the night, and I saw in the great chair at the bedside, Joe. I opened my eyes in the day and, sitting on the window-seat, smoking his pipe in the shaded open window, still I saw Joe. I asked for a cooling drink, and the dear hand that gave it to me was Joe's.') into a system for making sense of the whole book. Again, an exchange of ideas in the classroom might help the pupils to extend and refine their thinking. Several possibilities exist: having the chance to swap and explain their diagrams in small groups; building up a diagram together on the blackboard as a whole class group after individual explorations; selecting one or two particularly useful ones, putting them on the blackboard or photocopying enough to go round, and discussing them with the whole group; or perhaps the teacher could construct his own diagrams and ask the class, working in small groups, to challenge and question it. The real value of all these possible activities is to be found in the attempt to justify the decisions taken in the process of putting the diagram together. A wider and more precise pondering of the significance of the book's characters, patterns of behaviour, landscapes, images and conversations can often result from such activities.

TESTING IT AGAINST YOUR LIFE

Why don't you read what I have written and make up your own mind about what you think, *testing it against your own life, your own experience.* (Doris Lessing, from the preface to *The Golden Notebook*, London, Panther, 1973. *Author's italics*)

Getting inside a book like *Great Expectations* cannot be done without some kind of active, personal collaboration from the reader interweaving and mingling with it the experience of her own life. What the teacher can do is to encourage, at all times, the creation of personal contexts for the book, such as in this exploratory piece where a fifth-former weighs himself against Pip:

When Pip is in the middle of his expectations, he becomes snobby and takes a superior attitude to his lessers. I also sometimes take this attitude, but there is one big difference between me and Pip. Pip came by his superiority through fate and money; I came by mine through sheer hard work, in short, mine isn't based on money that can slip away like it did on Pip.

Whenever I sit any exam or test, the results only prove my point. Sometimes I am beaten but I don't really mind. There are times when I really don't want to be clever, as it only invited insults about how big headed I am, when it's the teacher who reads out my exam results, not me.

I am exposed to a sort of inverted snobbery, i.e. people less able than myself automatically assume that I'm just a big-headed freak whom you shouldn't be seen with and this is so annoying. It's so annoying that sometimes I just think, 'Oh, damn the lot of them' and look down on everyone just to ease the pressure a little.

Pip was fortunate in that he wasn't exposed to this and had a lot of good friends in the same position as himself, but I'm not quite so fortunate in this way. Either people don't understand what I say or the few who can do such wouldn't listen or aren't my friends at all. Therefore, the only person I can talk to who would understand is, believe it or not, myself. (No, I'm *not* mad, just in case you're wondering.) Hence, I take long slow walks on most nights to puzzle out problems, to work myself up for important events or to work out how to deal with excessive amounts of homework (which I may add, I receive frequently).

In the same sort of way, Pip and I have learnt the same lesson – 'it's not as nice as it looks at the top' only he could climb down, I can't.

(CHRIS FRANKS)

Chris is establishing a sense of himself and his own experience of being a clever fifth-form pupil in relation to some of the emotional pressures of the book, especially in chapters like the twenty-seventh one (Joe's visit to London) where '... Joe was rolling his eyes round and round the room, and round and round the flowered pattern of my dressing gown'.

He is putting his own feelings of pride ('... sheer hard work ...'), superiority and isolation against those of Pip and trying to build bridges between them, and also at the same time, pointing up the differences between the two experiences. Chris sees himself as the victim of a meritocratic system ('... it's the teacher who reads out my exam results, not me') and defines that against Pip's gaining of status 'through fate and money'. With directness and a baffled honesty he is seen in the process of taking the book on in terms of his current preoccupations.

Also Chris is learning to make explicit to himself and others the parallels between his experience and some of the book's concerns: '*In the same sort of way*, Pip and I have learnt the same lesson − "it's not as nice as it looks at the top" only he could climb down, I can't.'

FROM THE 'ME' TO THE 'THAT'

Our aim is to move dynamically from the 'me' of personal identification to the 'that' of the poem or the object in the poem. The discipline lies in the attentiveness to the 'that', and it should be made plain that there is no real dichotomy here, but a natural movement from subject to object and back again. (D.W. Harding, from 'Response to literature' in Margaret Meek, Aidan Warlow and Griselda Barton (eds), *The Cool Web*, London, Bodley Head, 1977)

From a position of personal confirmation (having gone, in some way, through these preliminary stages of understanding), pupils can move, often stumblingly, into the considered statement/examination essay/course work assignment hopefully without losing touch with the quality of the initial response. It is a difficult thing to do; very often the formal constraints of the examination essay scare pupils and teachers into hiding behind stock orthodoxies but, at best, some of the early flavour can be combined with more detailed evidence.

Here is one final example of a fifth-former adjusting to the rigours of the timed essay (forty minutes) two weeks before the examination:

What did Chapter 27 of *Great Expectations* mean to you and what is its importance in the design of the whole book?

The main storyline in the book is how Pip starts off humble, becomes a gentleman, and ends up almost his old self again. It is also how Pip starts off honest, becomes selfish and mean, and finishes honest again. The scene of Joe in London highlights this snobbery, and class division.

Even from the start Pip shows his true colours, although it may be unintentional, by describing the way Joe comes up the stairs. 'I knew it was Joe by the clumsy manner of coming up the stairs – his state boots being always too big for him – and by the time it took him to read the names on the other floors ...'. It's almost as if Pip's scorning him for having big boots, and not being able to read, and for generally not being as good as him. The next bit of (unintentional) snobbery was when Joe came into Pip's flat. Joe looks round the room, and at Pip's flowered dressing gown, and at the servant, and I think he's terribly over-awed. I say unintentional snobbery because I don't think Pip would dream of lording it over Joe, he just doesn't know he's doing it, which just goes to show how much of a snob he is.

The hat seems, to me, to play an important part in the scene. Joe won't give it to Pip, but holds it in front of him. When it is eventually coaxed away from him, he puts it where it keeps falling to the floor, yet before that Joe handled it delicately and carefully. Dickens described it as 'a bird's nest with eggs in'. Joe holds the hat between him and Pip, and is almost using it as a sheild [sic], to take refuge behind it. He is clinging on to it, and I think it is because it is a reminder from his world, and it is comfort in this alien, over-bearing world.

As I have said, the main theme of the book is social snobbery, and I see Pip as representing the snobby side, and Joe as the humble side. Joe shows how subordinate he feels by calling Pip 'Sir'. When Pip tells him off about that Joe looks at him 'with something faintly like reproach'. As if to say, 'You're better than me, with all these fancy things, I aught to respect you.'

But at the end, when they part, despite being a fish out of water, Joe finds it in him to be kind to Pip. This is one of the most touching bits in the book. It shows that you can be withouts airs and graces, and money and manners, and flowered dressing gowns, and servants, and still be honest, and kind and care for someone. This, for me, is the whole skeleton of the book, and that is why the scene is important.

There's some dutifulness here but there's also emerging confidence of tone and a personal, first person attack on the question existing, hand in hand, with a detailed attentiveness to the words on the page.

She's clearly been influenced by the Teacher's neat categories ('... the main theme of the book is social snobbery ...') but she is certainly on the way to making them her own and trusting in her own judgements. She is putting ideas in her own terms and often using her own informal language, like 'mean, snobby side', 'airs and graces', 'fish out of water', to see and summarize things for herself.

Not only is she focusing more sharply on particular incidents from the book to *prove* her case, but she is bringing together a perceptive commentary with a more engaged sensitivity. Take her handling of Joe's hat scene for instance. She effectively fits the scene into the book's overall structure (i.e. how low-status people find security in their dealings with an 'alien, over-bearing world') and, at the same time, investigates it in a way that suggests personal discovery: 'Joe holds the hat between him and Pip, and is almost using it as a sheild [sic], to take refuge behind it. He is clinging on to it, and I think it is because it is a reminder from his world...'.

There is an excited metaphorical adventurousness about the exploration here and in the last paragraph that is starting to unify critical intelligence and feeling that might profitably suggest some possible ways forward in the future.

NEW CONVERSATIONS, NEW TALK

If I've known a poem for some time and have already thought and talked about it rather thoroughly on previous occasions, I'm more at a disadvantage in any new conversation about it than at any advantage. If I can't forget all the things that I thought and said before, I certainly don't want to try and remember them more completely. If there's anything further I want to do with the poem now, it's to release my imagination to start from scratch with it and live it through again (John Newton, 'Literary Criticism, University Murder' from *The Cambridge Quarterly*, vol. 5, no. 4, 1971.)

Some teachers of literature are beginning to recognize fresh questions and challenges to their usual practice. How can we as teachers retain our genuine excitement about reading without swamping our pupils? Can we spot the right time for our telling to be constructively taken on by the pupils? Can we prevent our understandings from hardening out into the dead crust of rehearsed gestures for both pupils and teachers?

There are not any instant answers but, perhaps, if more teachers saw what they were doing in the classroom as the setting up of new conversations between pupils' experiences, the teacher's perceptions and the reading experience, rather than lectures about the book from the front, then we might have more chance of '... starting from scratch with it and (living) it through again...'.

If we can listen more attentively to the views of pupils who feel respected and valued and open up our classrooms to enable processes of understanding to take place more frequently then, again, we might find our pupils in a stronger position to create new words, in their talking and in their writing, about the books we ask them to read.

Notes

1 All page references are to the Penguin edition of *Great Expectations*.
2 See 'First Encounters', in *Children's Literature in Education*, Winter 1980; and 'Meeting books', in Mike Torbe (ed.), *Language, Teaching and Learning*, vol. 3: *English*, London, Ward Lock Educational, 1981.

PART THREE
FICTION FOR THE CLASSROOM

READING SUGGESTIONS FOR THE
FIRST PHASE – 11–12+
(FIRST YEAR – MIDDLE OF THE
SECOND YEAR)

Title	Author	Publisher
Private, Keep Out!	Gwen Grant	Fontana Lion
The Eighteenth Emergency	Betsy Byars	Puffin
Jacob Two-Two Meets the Hooded Fang	Mordecai Richler	Puffin
The Great Gilly Hopkins	Katherine Paterson	Puffin
The Turbulent Term of Tyke Tiler	Gene Kemp	Puffin
The Shrinking of Treehorn	F.P. Heide	Young Puffin
Challenge in the Dark	Robert Leeson	Fontana Young Lion
A Likely Place	Paula Fox	Piccolo/Pan
The Iron Man	Ted Hughes	Faber
Tales of a Fourth Grade Nothing	Judy Blume	Piccolo/Pan
Thunder and Lightnings	Jan Mark	Puffin
Third World Voices for Children	McDowell and Lavitt (eds)	Allison & Busby
The Battle of Bubble and Squeak	Philippa Pearce	Puffin
The Midnight Fox	Betsy Byars	Puffin
A Wizard of Earthsea	Ursula Le Guin	Puffin
Shadow Cage and Other Tales of the Supernatural	Philippa Pearce	Puffin
Philip Hall Likes Me, I Reckon, Maybe	Bette Green	Puffin
Conrad the Factory-Made Boy	Christine Nostlinger	Beaver Books

Title	Author	Publisher
A Northern Childhood: The Balaclava Story and Other Stories	George Layton	Longman Knockout
Old Dog, New Tricks	Dick Cate	Young Puffin
Skulker Wheat	John Griffin	Heinemann New Windmill
Orange, Yellow and Red Storyhouse	D. Jackson and D. Pepper (eds)	OUP
The Bakerloo Flea	Michael Rosen	Longman Knockout
Tales 1–5	Geoffrey Summerfield (ed.)	Ward Lock Educational
The Goalkeeper's Revenge and Other Stories	Bill Naughton	Puffin
From the Mixed Up Files of Mrs Basil E. Frankweiler	E.L. Konigsburg	Puffin
The Diddakoi	Rumer Godden	Puffin
The Dawnstone	Jill Paton Walsh	Piccolo/Pan

CLASS LIBRARY SUGGESTIONS FOR THE FIRST PHASE

Note: An attempt has been made to include picture story books, comic strip books and inventive information books in these Class Library lists to increase the range.

Title	Author	Publisher
The Peppermint Pig	Nina Bawden	Puffin
Playing it Right	Tony Drake	Puffin
The Wildman	Kevin Crossley-Holland	Andre Deutsch
Some Swell Pup	Matthew Margolis (illus. Maurice Sendak)	Picture Puffin
Asterix the Gaul	René Goscinny	Hodder & Stoughton/ Knight
The Stone Book Quartet	Alan Garner	Fontana Lion
Charlotte's Web	E.B. White	Puffin
Castle	David Macaulay	Collins
Not Now Bernard	David McKee	Hutchinson
How Tom Beat Captain Najork and his Hired Sportsmen	Russell Hoban (illus. Quentin Blake)	Picture Puffin
Peanuts	Charles Schulz	Coronet
How to Eat Fried Worms	Thomas Rockwell	Piccolo

Title	Author	Publisher
Danny the Champion of the World	Roald Dahl	Puffin
Flat Stanley	Jeff Brown	Methuen/Magnet
The Phantom Tollbooth	Norton Juster	Fontana Lion
Flying Free	Dick Cate	Beaver Books
Knock and Wait	Gwen Grant	Fontana Lion
Nasty!	Michael Rosen	Longman Knockout
Black Folktales	Julius Lester	Grove Press Inc., New York
Funny Folk: A Book of Comic Tales	Aidan Chambers	Fontana Lion
The TV Kid	Betsy Byars	Puffin
Grinny	Nicholas Fisk	Puffin
Gowie Corby Plays Chicken	Gene Kemp	Puffin
English Fairy Tales	Joseph Jacobs (ed.)	Bodley Head
The Summer of the Dinosaur	Willis Hall	Bodley Head
Grange Hill Rules O.K.?	Robert Leeson	Fontana Lion
Mrs Frisby and the Rats of NIMH	Robert C. O'Brien	Puffin
The Bonny Pit Laddie	Frederick Grice	Puffin
Bridge to Terabithia	Katherine Paterson	Puffin
What the Neighbours Did and Other Stories	Philippa Pearce	Puffin
Little House in the Big Woods (and others in the series)	Laura Ingalls Wilder	Puffin
It's Too Frightening For Me!	Shirley Hughes	Young Puffin
The Puffin Book of Improbable Records	Quentin Blake/Michael Yeoman	Young Puffin
Nothing To Be Afraid of	Jan Mark	Kestrel
Conrad's War	Andrew Davies	Scholastic Publications
Tintin in America	Hergé	Methuen/Magnet
Charlie and the Chocolate Factory	Roald Dahl	Puffin
Willie the Squowse	Ted Allan	Puffin
I'm Trying To Tell you	Bernard Ashley	Young Puffin
Haunted House	Jan Pienkowski	Heinemann
The Old Joke Book	J. & A. Ahlberg	Fontana Picture Lion

READING SUGGESTIONS FOR THE
SECOND PHASE – 12+–14

(UPPER SECOND YEAR–THIRD YEAR)

Title	Author	Publisher
Under Goliath	Peter Carter	Puffin
East End at Your Feet	Farrukh Dhondy	Macmillan Topliner
The Gates	Leslie Mildiner and Bill House	Centerprise
A Kind of Wild Justice	Bernard Ashley	Puffin
Daredevils or Scaredycats	Chris Powling	Fontana Lion
Mia	Gunnel Beckman	Longman Knockout
Across the Barricades	Joan Lingard	Puffin Plus
Slave Dancer	Paula Fox	Piccolo/Pan
Sweets from a Stranger	Nicholas Fisk	Kestrel
Teenage Encounters	Stella Ibekwe	Centerprise
Carrie's War	Nina Bawden	Puffin
Noah's Castle	John Rowe Townsend	Puffin Plus
Long Journey Home	Julius Lester	Longman Knockout
The Owl Service	Alan Garner	Fontana Lion
The Machine-Gunners	Robert Westall	Puffin
Joby	Stan Barstow	Heinemann New Windmill
Blue and Green Storyhouse	D. Jackson and D. Pepper (eds)	OUP
There Is a Happy Land	Keith Waterhouse	Longman Imprint
A Sillitoe Selection	Michael Marland (ed.)	Longman Imprint
A Pistol in Greenyards	Mollie Hunter	Piccolo/Pan
Alan and Naomi	Myron Levoy	Bodley Head
The Deserter	Nigel Gray	Fontana Lion
A Taste of Freedom	Julius Lester	Longman Knockout

Title	*Author*	*Publisher*
Elidor	Alan Garner	Fontana Lion
Killing Mr Griffin	Lois Duncan	Scholastic/Hippo
Animal Farm	George Orwell	Penguin
Late Night on Watling Street	Bill Naughton	Longman Imprint
Walkabout	J.V. Marshall	Puffin Plus
A Northern Childhood: The Fib And Other Stories	George Layton	Longman Knockout

CLASS LIBRARY SUGGESTIONS FOR
THE SECOND PHASE

Title	Author	Publisher
Skulls	Richard Steel	Piccolo/Pan
A Summer to Die	Lois Lowry	Dragon/Granada
Silver's Revenge	Robert Leeson	Collins
Prove Yourself a Hero	K.M. Peyton	Puffin Plus
The God Beneath the Sea	Edward Blishen and Leon Garfield	Longman
Underground	David Macaulay	Collins
The Magnet Book of Strange Tales	Jean Russell (ed.)	Methuen/Magnet
Fifteen	Beverly Cleary	Puffin
The Ghost on the Hill	John Gordon	Puffin Plus
Dockie	Martin Ballard	Fontana Lion
On the Run	Dick Cate	Macmillan Topliner
Nobody's Family Is Going To Change	Louise Fitzhugh	Fontana Lion
Flambards Trilogy	K.M. Peyton	Puffin
Let the Balloon Go	Ivan Southall	Puffin
Welcome Home, Jellybean	Marlene Fanta Shyer	Granada
Tom's Midnight Garden	Philippa Pearce	Puffin
Where the Wild Things Are	Maurice Sendak	Picture Puffin
Answering Miss Roberts	Christopher Leach	Macmillan Topliner
Come Away from the Water, Shirley	John Burningham	Jonathan Cape

Title	Author	Publisher
The Wave and Other Stories	Liam O'Flaherty	Longman Imprint
Gangs and Victims	John Foster (ed.)	Nelson Getaway
The Ghost of Thomas Kempe	Penelope Lively	Piccolo/Pan
The King of the Barbareens	Janet Hitchman	Puffin Plus
Tracks and Signs	N. Tinbergen and E.A.R. Ennion	OUP
Ask Me No Questions	Ann Schlee	Puffin
Sea-Stranger, Fire-Brother and Earth-Father	Kevin Crossley-Holland	Piccolo/Pan
Railway Passage	Charles Keeping	OUP
Mischling, Second Degree	I. Koehn	Puffin Plus
Break of Dark	Robert Westall	Chatto & Windus
Song for a Dark Queen	Rosemary Sutcliff	Knight/Hodder & Stoughton
The Exeter Blitz	David Rees	Dragon/Granada
The Mouse and His Child	Russell Hoban	Puffin
Tig's Crime	T.R. Burch	Fontana Lion
I Was There	Hans Peter Richter	Kestrel

READING SUGGESTIONS FOR THE
THIRD PHASE – 14–16
(FOURTH AND FIFTH YEARS)

Title	Author	Publisher
The Fox in Winter	John Branfield	Fontana Lion
Basketball Game	Julius Lester	Puffin Plus
Z for Zachariah	Robert C. O'Brien	Fontana Lion/ Heinemann New Windmill
Looks and Smiles	Barry Hines	Michael Joseph/ Longman Imprint
It's My Life	Robert Leeson	Fontana Lion
A Sense of Shame and Other Stories	Jan Needle	Fontana Lion
Go Well, Stay Well	Toeckey Jones	Fontana Lion
A Very Long Way From Anywhere Else	Ursula Le Guin	Puffin Plus
A Comprehensive Education	Roger Mills	Centerprise
Ways of Sunlight	Samuel Selvon	Longman
Collision Course	Nigel Hinton	Puffin
I am The Cheese	Robert Cormier	Fontana Lion
Hiroshima	John Hersey	Penguin
Come to Mecca and Other Stories	Farrukh Dhondy	Fontana Lion
Sliding	Leslie Norris	Longman Imprint
The Intruder	John Rowe Townsend	Puffin Plus
Black Boy	Richard Wright	Longman Imprint

Title	Author	Publisher
Sticks and Stones	Susan Price	Faber
Our Lives: Young People's Autobiographies	Several	ILEA English Centre
To Kill a Mockingbird	Harper Lee	Heinemann New Windmill
Kes	Barry Hines	Penguin
A Hemingway Selection	Dennis Pepper (ed.)	Longman Imprint
Company K	William March	Nelson Getaway
Through the Wilderness	Dan Jacobson	Penguin
The L-Shaped Room	L.R. Banks	Penguin
A Casual Acquaintance	Stan Barstow	Longman Imprint
The Spitfire Grave	John Gordon	Kestrel
The Wave	Morton Rhue	Puffin Plus

CLASS LIBRARY SUGGESTIONS FOR
THE THIRD PHASE

Title	Author	Publisher
Love You, Hate You, Just Don't Know	Josie Karavasil (ed.)	Scholastic/Hippo
You Can't Keep Out the Darkness	Peggy Woodford (ed.)	Bodley Head
The Waterfall Box	John Gordon	Kestrel
My Darling, My Hamburger	Paul Zindel	Fontana Lion
Edith Jackson	Rosa Guy	Gollancz
A Temporary Open Air Life	Christopher Leach	Macmillan Topliner
Fungus the Bogeyman	Raymond Briggs	Picture Puffin
Nineteen Is too Young To Die	Gunnel Beckman	Macmillan Topliner
Dinky Hocker Shoots Smack!	M.E. Kerr	Puffin
Fair Fight	Barry Pointon	Longman Knockout
Roll of Thunder, Hear My Cry	Mildred D. Taylor	Puffin
The Son of Someone Famous	M.E. Kerr	Puffin
After the First Death	Robert Cormier	Fontana Lion
When the Wind Blows	Raymond Briggs	Hamish Hamilton
Girls Are Powerful	Susan Hemmings (ed.)	Sheba
The Outsiders	S.E. Hinton	Fontana Lion

Title	Author	Publisher
Is Anyone There?	Monica Dickens and Rosemary Sutcliffe (eds)	Puffin
The Summer After the Funeral	Jane Gardam	Peacock
The Wild Washerwomen	Michael Yeoman and Quentin Blake	Picture Puffin
The Human Element and Other Stories	Stan Barstow	Longman Imprint
Only a Game	Eamon Dunphy	Puffin
Nancekuke	John Branfield	Hutchinson Educational
World Zero Minus	A. & N. Chambers (eds)	Macmillan Topliner
The Habit of Loving	Doris Lessing	Panther
Miguel Street	V.S. Naipaul	Penguin
My Oedipus Complex and Other Stories	Frank O'Connor	Penguin
Catcher in the Rye	J.D. Salinger	Penguin
Of Mice and Men	John Steinbeck	Heinemann New Windmill
The Real Thing	Peggy Woodford (ed.)	Puffin Plus
Summer's End	Archie Hill	Wheaton (Exeter)
Tales of the Unexpected	Roald Dahl	Penguin
Twopence a Tub	Susan Price	Faber
Poona Company	Farrukh Dhondy	Gollancz
Shadows on our Skin	Jennifer Johnston	Hodder & Stoughton/ Coronet Books